SUE MONK
KIDD

SUE MONK KIDD

A COLLECTION OF CRITICAL ESSAYS

FOREWORD BY SUE MONK KIDD

EDITED BY
DEBORAH J. KUHLMANN

FORT WORTH, TEXAS

Library of Congress Cataloging-in-Publication Data

Names: Kuhlmann, Deborah Jane, 1947- editor, author. | McClenagan, Cindy, author.
| Heath, Erin (Erin C.), author. | Mayfield, Arch, 1948- author. | Kidd, Sue
Monk, writer of foreword. | McClenagan, Cindy. Postcolonialism and the pursuit
of identity in The invention of wings.
Title: Sue Monk Kidd : a collection of critical essays / edited by Deborah J. Kuhlmann.
Description: Fort Worth : TCU Press, [2023] | Includes bibliographical references. |
Summary: "In keeping with the traditional academic genre of collected essays, Sue
Monk Kidd: A Collection of Critical Essays offers seven analytic studies of several
of Kidd's novels, including The Invention of Wings, The Secret Life of Bees and
The Book of Longings plus the film version of The Secret Life of Bees to bring
expanded perspectives to her work for avid readers as well as academics. These literary essays can serve as examples for students of literature, find a place in college
English classrooms as well as libraries for both secondary and higher education,
and appeal to scholars of American literature.—Provided by publisher.
Identifiers: LCCN 2022047230 (print) | LCCN 2022047231 (ebook) | ISBN
9780875658155 (paperback) | ISBN 9780875658445 (ebook)
Subjects: LCSH: Kidd, Sue Monk—Criticism and interpretation. | American essays—
Texas. | LCGFT: Essays.
Classification: LCC PS3611.I44 Z86 2023 (print) | LCC PS3611.I44 (ebook) |
DDC 813/.6--dc23/eng/20221004
LC record available at https://lccn.loc.gov/2022047230
LC ebook record available at https://lccn.loc.gov/2022047231

TCU Box 298300
Fort Worth, Texas 76129

Design by Preston Thomas

DEDICATION

TO SUE MONK KIDD,

BS, Texas Christian University, 1970
Honorary Doctorate of Letters, Texas Christian University, 2016

CONTENTS

FOREWORD

Over the years, I've heard from countless readers describing their experiences of reading my novels. Encountering the response of literary scholars to my work, however, is a brave new world.

Lay readers tend to read a work of fiction through the lens of their *own* experience, that is, to assimilate the work in the context of their personal world, coming to understand it through the sieve of their particular need, identity, life experience, and worldview at the time. I've heard from readers who experienced *The Secret Life of Bees,* first and foremost, as a story about a motherless girl and her quest for belonging and love, while others told me that, above all, it is a story about racial injustice and the struggle for civil rights. Still others wrote to me indicating that the real essence of the novel is the spirituality and sisterhood of black women. The varying list of responses to the story goes on.

At the same time, paradoxically, we read through the lens of the *other's* experience. In what is surely one of the most mysterious human transactions, we leave ourselves, fly to some other sky, and drop into the lives of the characters. Through empathetic participation we become the character for a while, experiencing the world as she does, seeing it with her eyes and feeling it with her heart.

When I finish writing a novel and send it to the publisher, I am filled with a deep sense of relinquishment, with the sense that I've done all I can and now the story belongs to the readers. It becomes a new creation through their experience of it. Until I read the exceptional essays in this book, it had seemed that my novels found their life, their real being through those two seemingly contradictory approaches—reading through the lens of personal experience and the lens of empathic participation. But somewhere in the midst of these pages, I realized there was a third lens, the keen, multifocal lens of the scholar through which a novel is read into being in its own unique way.

In the essay, "On Studies," Francis Bacon wrote:

> Some books are to be tasted, others to be swallowed, and some few to be chewed and digested: that is, some books are to be read only in parts; others to be read, but not curiously; and some few to be read wholly and with diligence and attention.

The scholars represented in these pages did not taste or swallow my work, so much as chew and digest it. They read wholly, with diligence and attention. The lens through which they read was more like a prism that splits whatever light my novels give off into otherwise unseen colors. My novels became more vivid for it. The hidden inner workings were revealed. Even to me.

In the early drafts of my fiction, I write more or less unconsciously, following not the dictates of my opinionated, rational mind, but giving myself over to the whims of my imagination, as well as to some unknown choreographer, who exists offstage in the nether region of my thoughts, creating the meticulous movements of the story, turning them into a cohesive dance. Even if I don't understand what this choreographer is up to, I trust her. It is only later that I consult with my conscious mind and its team of inner advisers, editors, critics, and craft persons. Because so much of my writing goes on in the murky depths of creativity, I'm grateful for the analyses, insights, and revelations of these literary scholars. It was eye-opening, for instance, to read in one of the essays that the humor in *The Secret Life of Bees* could be understood as female subversion, causing me to recognize what I'd been attempting to do beneath the surface of my own awareness.

The essays in this book are something of a wonder to me, not only for the scholarship brought to bear on my novels and for what it unveils, but for the way the scholars themselves have read my work forward, bringing it further into being.

—SUE MONK KIDD

Sue Monk Kidd, a 1970 graduate of TCU, is the author of nine books, including her debut novel, *The Secret Life of Bees.* Translated into thirty-six languages, the award-winning novel spent more than two-and-a-half years on the *New York Times* bestseller list and was turned into a major motion picture and an Off-Broadway musical. Kidd's novel *The Mermaid Chair,* winner of the Quill Award, was a number one *New York Times* bestseller and adapted into a television movie. *The Invention of Wings,* Kidd's third nov-el, also reached number one on the *New York Times* bestseller list, was an Oprah's Book Club pick, and received the SIBA award and Florida Book Award. Her latest novel, *The Book of Longings,* another *New York Times* bestseller, was published to widespread critical acclaim and translated into seventeen languages. Her memoirs include *The Dance of the Dissident Daughter* and *Traveling with Pomegranates,* cowritten with her daughter, Ann Kidd Taylor. Kidd has been inducted into the South Carolina Academy of Authors and the Georgia Writers Hall of Fame. TCU conferred an Honorary Doctor of Letters on her in 2016. She lives in North Carolina.

INTRODUCTION

S ue Monk Kidd's work is well rooted in the wrestling with big questions literature through the ages has addressed. What does it mean to be human? How does one approach the mystery and power of the Creator? To what extent are love and truth and freedom and forgiveness intertwined? Is the past ever past? Can healing happen? And yet, perhaps this is the reason her writings invite scholars and critics to view her work through varied lenses. Still, while the Kidd perspective may be seen as poetic, adolescent, historical, ontological, theological, feminist, psychological, mythological, postmodern, Christian, post-Christian, postcolonial, and more, she is most essentially a southern novelist. Having been born and raised in Georgia and placing the setting of most of her fiction in the American South, this heritage is undeniable. Moreover, her novels, particularly *The Invention of Wings* and *The Secret Life of Bees*, lend themselves to capturing the imagination in such a way that they easily inhabit the canon of southern literature.

Like William Faulkner, Kate Chopin, Tennessee Williams, Alice Walker, Carson McCullers, Flannery O'Connor, Zora Neale Hurston, Harper Lee, and other notable southern authors before her, Sue Monk Kidd's vision is more tragedy than morality play or melodrama, close to Realism but not without Romanticism. Oppression, abuse, abandonment, injustice, and human tragedies, not to be ignored, find their way into her novels, where they are met not with an easy or tension-free resolution, and yet love, humor, insight, transcendence, and grit are rendered in the face of inhumane difficulties. As Alice Walker said in "Beyond the Pea-cock: The Reconstruction of Flannery O'Connor," "'Well,' I say, 'I believe that the truth about any subject only comes when all the sides of the story are put together, and all their different meanings make one new one. Each writer writes the missing parts to the oth-er writer's story. And the whole story is what I'm after.'"[1] Likewise, the works of Sue Monk Kidd invent and present oppositions, cre-ate parallel worlds, and invent different perspectives and, therefore, provide the possibility for a more totally intact and complete truth to be told.

Courtney George in "Why and How I Teach Southern Liter-ature: A Work in Progress" expands on this "whole story" quota-tion, saying that Walker was writing "about southern women and their contributions, but [she was] also writing about systemic and institutionalized injustices because individual stories and (literary) canons are formed within the framework of systems and institu-tions, thus that framework informs how the 'whole story' is written and studied."[2] Kidd, too, revisits in her novels the institutionalized racism and slavery of the past as well as the enduring relationships between races that were and always have been part of southern his-tory, even in the midst of trauma. Here in the midst of extremities she rightfully claims her spot in the canon of southern literature.

This collection of critical essays, focusing on several texts, re-veals similar visions in her works that see a world in which it is possible for disintegration to lead to wholeness for human beings. Such triumph that arises out the ashes of tragedy is itself a motif in southern literature. We are reminded of William Faulkner's famous quotation from his Nobel Prize speech "that man will not merely endure: he will prevail."[3] Such is any victory in the world of par-adoxes and polar opposites that inhabit the fiction of Sue Monk Kidd, as she reaches to tell not a partial but a complete tale.

In the southern literary tradition in which her novels fall, struggle and tragedy are felt by all of her characters. She follows Faulkner and others who write about "the problems of the human heart in conflict with itself."[4] Ultimately, however, her plots thread their way in time to a space where a synthesis of such dichotomies is both possible and probable. For instance, in both *The Invention of Wings* and *The Secret Life of Bees,* that which is invisible is made visible, that which originates in consciousness makes its way to materiality, that which begins in darkness moves into the light, that which is mysterious nevertheless eventually manifests in the most obvious and mundane of ways, and that which is most grounded possesses the power to fly. Kidd's perspective sees truth itself as paradoxical, always a dialectical dance of opposites that resists any certainty of being merely one or the other, black or white.

My hope is that these essays will touch the imagination and invite more investigation into Kidd's fiction and nonfiction, which deserve more scholarly attention than they have received at this point. This study takes various approaches to what it means to be a southern writer, and including Kidd in the canon may provide a new approach to her work.

Identity in the literature of the South, a geographic region that itself has struggled with social, cultural, historical, and linguistic questions of identity, is not dissimilar to postcolonial literature that often addresses the same issue. Lucinda MacKethan, in "Genres of Southern Literature," observes that Zora Neale Hurston's *Their Eyes Were Watching God* does not "gloss over the racial oppression associated with the southern rural landscape, but [asserts simultaneously] that a search for inheritance and sustenance within a southern past is essential to the attainment of full identity."[5] Sue Monk Kidd's *The Invention of Wings* delivers the same. Both plot and characters unite the conflicts and contrasts that must intersect and integrate in order to tell the whole story or provide an authentic identity.

In "Postcolonialism and the Pursuit of Identity in Kidd's *The Invention of Wings,*" Cindy McClenagan examines Kidd's novel as an adolescent search for identity akin to the postcolonial quest for self. Kidd's most recent novel focuses on the lives of two nineteenth-century South Carolinian females of similar age but of vastly different classes: Hetty, or "Handful," is a slave, while Sarah is a slaveholder's daughter. McClenagan asserts that Kidd's novel demonstrates how postcolonial literature and young adult literature can intersect in their "presentation of the search for identity, as both exhibit a rebuilding self in the 'shadow of a dominating force.'" As the novel progresses, Handful's growth mirrors Erik H. Erikson's theory of young adult development, culminating in her rejection of the traditional limits placed on her by the culture of the South. Thus, she ultimately defies those definitions as she dares to take on self-construction in a southern "world not of [her] own making." To a large extent, then, Handful embodies MacKethan's view that

> southern women . . . African American and white, might be expected to have had problems finding empowerment within the context of images of land and traditional order. Yet from Kate Chopin and Ellen Glasgow as transitional figures of great importance, to Hurston, Elizabeth Madox Roberts, Eudora Welty, Katherine Anne Porter and Harriet Arnow, southern women writers have returned to, revised, and revitalized the meaning of women's relationship to the land and to tradition.[6]

McClenagan's study of identity puts Kidd in good company with these earlier southern revisionists, as Handful's adolescent identity development aligns with the postcolonial emphasis on self-construction through revision of cultural tradition.

Moreover, these characters are fueled by the belief that it is possible to choose and claim one's right to liberation, even though such an endeavor requires taking the road less travelled to self-knowledge and personal truth in a world of oppression, persecution, enslavement, and exploitation. Where freedom ultimately resides for Kidd is internal. The oppositions that may have been generated by external influences eventually come to reside within the hearts and minds of human beings, so that is where the reckoning must originate, if there is to be any chance at all to garner true freedom. Metaphors of flying inhabit both novels, *Wings* and *The Secret Life of Bees*, but the possibility of soaring begins in the imagination. For

Kidd, liberation is an inner, spiritual choice that precedes releasing any physical or mental chains that may hold a person back from expressing and executing her/his full humanity.

As I discuss in "A Flying Leap of Faith," *The Invention of Wings* ends with the two women ready to cross the river, where they are perched on the edge of the unknown and the promise of freedom, but it takes a flying leap of faith to take the risk. The novel at that very moment places Kidd's imagery close to that of Flannery O'Conner, who William Ness suggests in "'Getting Somewhere': Motion and Stasis in The Works of Flannery O'Connor" that

> where we are going in an O'Connor story is a place of trans-
> formation, of revelation, of grace. This "place" may or may not
> have a geographical contingency involved. How we arrive does
> matter, but the grace encounter may come to the characters of
> its own accord or otherwise take them by surprise. Protagonists
> seldom know that they are going toward such an encounter,
> and even when they do have some inkling that they are bound
> for transformation, they have little foreknowledge of what the
> experience will entail.[7]

Moreover, they stand on the edge of the river, ready to cross, evoking what Glenda Weathers in "Biblical Trees, Biblical Deliverance: Literary Landscapes of Zora Neale Hurston and Toni Morrison" reports as a powerful metaphor for African American writers, southern or not.

> Enslaved by law or custom, African Americans have found
> the Promised Land metaphor an apt vehicle for describing the
> epic proportion of their suffering. Using this metaphor, they
> can identify with the Old Testament Israelites who were under
> God's special providence. When read typologically, their per-
> secutions offer evidence that they are God's new chosen who,
> like the biblical Jews, can hope for a better life in a different
> place—a land attainable by a "flight out of Egypt," implying
> a "crossing over" the Red Sea or its symbolic equivalent. Black

vernacular songs such as "Bound for the Promised Land," "Going Into Canaan," "I Won't Have to Cross Jordan Alone," and "Go Down Moses" attest to the metaphor's power for engendering hope.[8]

Furthermore, the Promised Land evokes "an imaginative place on the other side of some barrier—often a river—that must be crossed for deliverance."[9] By placing her characters on the edge of this river as they dare to capture their freedom together, Kidd achieves a synthesis of characters from opposite worlds united in a moment of grace, a leap of faith, and a promise of deliverance. And she achieves a synthesis via her imagery that would find affinity with other southern writers, specifically both O'Connor and Hurston.

When viewing *The Invention of Wings* through a historical lens, it is clear that the dilemmas faced both by women and slaves are intertwined. The journey to adulthood of Handful and Sarah is a process of self-invention that demands great courage as it defies the heavily entrenched patriarchal structures that Kidd implies need revision or reinvention.

In her 2008 article entitled "Reclamation in Walker's *Jubilee*: The Context of Development of the Historical Novel," Babacar Dieng finds that when Margaret Walker, who spent all of her early life in Alabama, wrote *Jubilee*, Walker's years of unremitting research contributed to her discovery that

> white southern historians and novelists misrepresented the
> process and institution of enslavement. They claimed it was a
> beneficial system with benign masters. As for Northerners, they
> did not oppose enslavement as long as it was "contained" in
> the South and did not spread into the territories. With *Jubilee*,
> Walker wanted to revise history to accommodate a valid Black
> perspective and to revive the African American memory swept
> away by these master-narratives. As she explains in *How I Wrote
> Jubilee*, she planned to write a folk novel so as to capture the
> true experience and cultural memory of the enslaved and to
> show the significance of Black people and their role during the

war, because these aspects had been blotted out of the dominant culture's representations (26). Additionally, Walker wanted to tell the story from a Black woman's perspective because she felt that "the black woman's story has not been told, has not been dealt adequately" (Giovanni 55). She felt that the historical novel would be the most suitable way to teach people about a time and a place as they "are more inclined to read fiction than history" (Rowell 23).[10]

This is not to say that Sue Monk Kidd's 2014 historical novel, which seeks to retell the story of abolitionist Sarah Grimké, reaches to validate a Black perspective, but Kidd does share Walker's approach to revisionist history, as Kidd portrays both Sarah, the slaveholder's daughter, and Handful, the slave, overcoming any history in which white southern writers depict slavery as beneficial, while also teaching her readers through fiction more of the truth of the historical experience of southern women.

In "A Life Story," a lecture she gave at the Westminster Forum in 2014, Kidd states that she always wants her readers to have *empathy*.[11] Thus, the related question asks what informs this very primary value of hers. Given her roots in the Judeo-Christian tradition, it would be pertinent to ask if her theological outlook, present in most all of her works, gives rise to the perspective expressed in the film version of *The Secret Life of Bees*. Erin Heath finds in "She May Bee Like Jesus: African American Female Christ Figure in *The Secret Life of Bees*" that a "consistently black female-centered approach to Christianity" is a central foundation upon which the film of Kidd's book rests. Heath argues that the character "with a non-normative mental state serves as the Christ figure," a definite move away from but informed by traditional American Christianity. Furthermore, Heath sees this "feminized non-neurotypical African American Christian narrative" as the bedrock for the novel's "significant message of inclusivity, acceptance, and empathy." Heath's insights then make it arguable that Kidd's work finds a firm position in the southern canon next to Flannery O'Connor, another writer whose theology was interwoven in her fiction and who, according to Di Renzo, quoted by Maria Bloshteyn in "Dostoevsky and the Literature of the American South,"

> believes that her characters need to experience suffering first-hand if they are ever to become authentic in an unjust world. The pain of being mortal and vulnerable is the one thing that teaches them pity and humility. This stark compassion, this Christ-like identification with the insulted and the injured, becomes possible in O'Connor's fiction only when her characters are broken. (Di Renzo, "American Gargoyles: Flannery O'Connor and the Medieval Grotesque," 41–42)[12]

Heath's exploration of *The Secret Life of Bees* reveals how Kidd, like other southern authors, including O'Connor, reveals that there is nothing insane about the notion that love is possible out of ruins, resurrection can come out of sacrifice, and suffering is redemptive.

Likewise, in "Secrets of Being in Sue Monk Kidd's *The Secret Life of Bees*," I use an ontological lens, even an epistemological, phenomenological, and theological one, to examine *Bees* as a study of the terrain any pilgrim in pursuit of an expanded consciousness must cross, which most definitely includes crossings and conflicts that require reconciliation. An essential mystery resides in *The Secret Life of Bees*, and the novel's focus is about finding spiritual sanctuary in being itself. However, in a near St. Augustinian sense, Kidd creates characters who embody the ancient recognition of the human need to worship, and seeking the peace that passes present understanding, the characters create a service based on Christian litany. In a theological reversal of sorts, their savior is ironically or paradoxically feminine, suggesting a theological hybrid, if you will, that is not so much post Christian as Christian based. Clearly for Kidd, again, the imagination rules, and the intersecting of opposing mindsets abound, as this story of being southern is told in its entirety.

Now, Maria Bloshteyn reminds us that it was Flannery O'Connor who argued that the southern grotesques arise out of the author's need to combine two disparate things, saying that

> the grotesque is only a "symptom" of a theological vision of
> society, history, and the human being that is especially prev-
> alent in the South. In order to create a grotesque, she insists,
> "you have to have some conception of the whole man, and in
> the South the general conception of man is still, in the main,
> theological" (44).[13]

While Kidd does not write a southern grotesque novel, *Bees* most
definitely finds kinship with O'Connor's conception of man in
southern literature as theological. Moreover, according to O'Connor,
"Christian faith or, at least, struggles with this faith have always been
of great importance in the South."[14] And finally, O'Connor even
points out in the most famous statement made about the place of
religion in the South since H. L. Mencken condescendingly called
it the Bible Belt, "I think it is safe to say that while the South is
hardly Christ-centered, it is most certainly Christ-haunted" (44).[15]
Kidd's work could arguably be included, as the spiritual services in
The Secret Life of Bees, portrayed as necessary to wholeness, are both
informed by Christianity and at the same time recognize the need
for solace, sanctuary, and worship to be re-envisioned, if they are
to resonate with congregants. Such a redemptive reconciliation is a
hallmark of Kidd's southern novel.

   As I discuss in "The Power of Poetic Perception in *The Secret Life
of Bees,*" Kidd is a poet and lyrical image-maker. In light of *The Poetics
of Space* by Gaston Bachelard, who finds that "Contemporary poetry
. . . has introduced freedom in the very body of the language. [And,]
as a result, poetry appears as a phenomenon of freedom,"[16] I believe
that the protagonist in *The Secret Life of Bees* finds her freedom in
her poetic perception, which renders the world around her in rich
and vivid detail. Bachelard maintains that images themselves hold a
"poetic significance," [for] "poetry is there with its countless surging
images, images through which the creative imagination comes to live
in its own domain."[17] In *The Secret Life of Bees* poetic images abound
in the "shimmering consciousness" and imagination of Lily Owens,

from whose point of view her secrets—and secrets of being itself in an ontological sense—are revealed. Confirming her own spirituality in an interview in 2006, Kidd speaks of what she calls "deep being."[18] It is this being that is mirrored in the poetic images in *The Secret Life of Bees*, and where the character finds the freedom that has been within herself all along.

In this affirmation of the poetic imagination as a means to understanding, Kidd joins another southern writer, Robert Penn Warren. Indeed, Lesa Carnes Corrigan finds that in "Knowledge and the Image of Man" Warren advanced his personal creed that

> "poetry—that is, literature as a dimension of the creative
> imagination—is knowledge." Echoing Wordsworth's assertion
> in the 1800 Preface to *Lyrical Ballads* that "poetry is the breath
> and finer spirit of all knowledge," Warren extends his Romantic
> correlative into a reconciliation of opposites, submitting his
> view that "poetry . . . [springs] from the deep engagement of
> spirit with the world."[19]

Similarly, in her poetic voice embodied by Lily in *The Secret Life of Bees*, Kidd offers her own correlative found in pure being that unites fully and engages wholly with life, a tribute to the imagination from yet another Southern Romantic perspective.

In "Humor and the Art of Survival in Sue Monk Kidd's *The Secret Life of Bees*," Arch Mayfield delivers keen insight into how Lily, the protagonist, uses humor for sheer survival. Identifying her ability to cope with the hypocrisies of society, Mayfield names her humor as resilient, evoking Mark Twain's Huckleberry Finn and provoking possible further consideration of Kidd as social critic. Occasionally, Lily's humor is, says Mayfield, scatological, again securing a space for Sue Monk Kidd among southern humorists. In *Comic Visions, Female Voice: Contemporary Women Novelists and Southern Humor* Barbara Bennett asserts that

> humor is an intricate part of many southern women writers'
> works, helping to define voice, communicate theme, and estab-

lish new definitions of southern literature; the tone is often more optimistic and less guilt ridden than that found in fiction written by men or by their literary predecessors. In addition, most female humor has a distinct voice and vision: iconoclastic, yet ultimately unifying; challenging traditional relationships, yet affirming the self and family.[20]

This unification of polarities and affirmations of paradoxes is evident in Kidd's contribution to southern humor, which becomes a way to tell a whole story of the South.

Gregory Donovan, in "Several Denials and a Few Confessions: Southern Poetry and Southern Journals," reminds us that "Historian C. Hugh Holman . . . theorized in *The Immoderate Past: the Southern Writer and History* that . . . the South's imagination was characteristically dialectical and thus historical (while the North's imagination, rooted in Puritan ideals, was typological and ahistorical)."[21] Though they may be viewed from various literary perspectives, Sue Monk Kidd's novels, particularly *The Secret Life of Bees* and *The Invention of Wings*, will find critics from any angle ultimately seeing a dialectical dance of opposites in a revisited past, be it a personal or a historical one, so that they join the southern imagination of which Holman speaks. Donovan goes on to say:

We are all quite familiar with Faulkner's formulation, through his character Gavin Stevens in *Requiem for a Nun*, that "the past is not dead. It's not even past." Such a formulation is far from Nietzsche's recommended pathway to happiness of "active forgetting." It is not an evasion of history; it is an embrace of it—ultimately, all of it.[22]

The works of Sue Monk Kidd, including her most recent novel *The Book of Longings*, likewise reach to tell "all of it," the "whole story," as would be the case for any southern or for that matter any writer whose works would make the human being and his/her human story what matters most. And therein lies the heart of Kidd's texts and their timeless appeal.

NOTES

1. Courtney George, "Why and How I Teach Southern Literature, A Work in Progress," *South, A Scholarly Journal* 50.2 (2018): 135, Academic Search Complete http://search.ebscohost.com.waylandbu.idm.oclc.org/login.aspx?direct=true&db=a9h&AN=135571193&site=eds-live.
2. George, "Why and How I Teach Southern Literature," 138-139.
3. William Faulkner, "William Faulkner Banquet Speech," The Nobel Prize, accessed September 3, 2019, https://www.nobelprize.org/prizes/literature/1949/faulkner/speech/.
4. Faulkner, "Speech."
5. Lucinda MacKethan, "Genres of Southern Literature," *Southern Spaces* (2004): https://www.nobelprize.org/prizes/literature/1949/faulkner/speech/.
6. MacKethan, "Genres."
7. William Ness, "'Getting Somewhere': Motion and Stasis in the Works of Flannery O'Connor," *Renascence* (2): 99, http://search.ebscohost.com.waylandbu.idm.oclc.org/login.aspx?direct=true&db=a9h&AN=123550122&site=eds-live.
8. Glenda Weathers, "Biblical Trees, Biblical Deliverance: Literary Landscapes of Zora Neale Hurston and Toni Morrison," *African American Review* 39 (1/2): 201, http://search.ebscohost.com.waylandbu.idm.oclc.org/login.aspx?direct=true&db=a9h&AN=18394221&site=eds-live.
9. Weathers, "Biblical Trees, Biblical Deliverance," 201.
10. Babacar Dieng, "Reclamation in Walker's Jubilee, The Context of Development of the Historical Novel," *Journal of Pan African Studies*, 2: 4 (2008): 125, http://search.ebscohost.com.waylandbu.idm.oclc.org/login.aspx?direct=true&db=a9h&AN=32926377&site=eds-live.
11. Sue Monk Kidd, "Life Is a Story," YouTube video, 00:60, from Westminster Forum February 11, 2014, posted by MySPNN, February 25, 2014, https://www.youtube.com/watch?v=152Prmb1IK8.
12. Maria Bloshteyn, "Dostoevsky and the Literature of the American South," *Southern Literary Journal* 37.1 (2004): 17, doi:10.1353/slj.2005.0002.
13. Bloshteyn, "Dostoevsky," 9.
14. Bloshteyn, "Dostoevsky," 9.
15. Bloshteyn, "Dostoevsky," 9.
16. Gaston Bachelard, *The Poetics of Space*, trans. Maria Jolas (New York: Penguin, 2014), 12.
17. Bachelard, *The Poetics of Space*, 13.
18. Cindy Crossby, "PW Talks with Sue Monk Kidd Remembering the Spirit,"

Publishers Weekly 253.27 (2006): 73, Literature Resource
Center, http://eds.a.ebscohost.com.yosemite.wbu.edu/eds/results?
vid=0&sid=782741a978dc4600b1f139b7162632f1%40sessionmgr4008&
bquery=TI+((Sue+AND+Monk+AND+Kidd+AND+Remembering+
AND+the+AND+Spirit))&bdata=JmNsaTA9RlQmY2x2MD1ZJnR5c-
GU9MCZzaXRlPWVkcy1saXZl.

19. Lesa Carnes Corrigan, *Poems of Pure Imagination: Robert Penn Warren and
the Romantic Tradition* (Baton Rouge: Louisiana State University Press,
1999), 17, http://search.ebscohost.com.waylandbu.idm.oclc.org/login.
aspx?direct=true&db=nlebk&AN=42497&site=eds-live.

20. Barbara Bennett, *Comic Visions, Female Voices : Contemporary Women Novelists and Southern Humor* (Baton Rouge: Louisiana State University Press,
1998), 2, http://search.ebscohost.com.waylandbu.idm.oclc.org/login.
aspx?direct=true&db=nlebk&AN=45662&site=eds-live.

21. Gregory Donovan, "Several Denials and a Few Confessions: Southern
Poetry and Southern Journals," *Southern Quarterly* 45 (1): 14, http://
search.ebscohost.com.waylandbu.idm.oclc.org/login.aspx?direct=true&
db=a9h&AN=28439978&site=eds-live.

22. Donovan, "Several Denials and a Few Confessions," 14.

BIBLIOGRAPHY

Bachelard, Gaston. *The Poetics of Space.* Translated by Maria Jolas. New York:
Penguin, 2014.

Bennett, Barbara. *Comic Visions, Female Voices : Contemporary Women Novelists and Southern Humor.* Baton Rouge: Louisiana State University Press,
1998. http://search.ebscohost.com.waylandbu.idm.oclc.org/login.aspx?di-
rect=true&db=nlebk&AN=42497&site=eds-live.

Bloshteyn, Maria. "Dostoevksy and the Literature of the American South."
Southern Literary Journal 37.1 (2004): 1-23. doi:10.1353/slj.2005.0002.

Corrigan, Lea Carnes. *Poems of Pure Imagination: Robert Penn Warren and
the Romantic Tradition.* Baton Rouge: Louisiana State University Press,
1999. http://search.ebscohost.com.waylandbu.idm.oclc.org/login.aspx?di-
rect=true&db=nlebk&AN=42497&site=eds-live.

Crossby, Cindy. "PW Talks with Sue Monk Kidd Remembering the Spirit."
Publishers Weekly 253, no. 27 (2006): 73. Literature Resource Center.
http://eds.a.ebscohost.com.yosemite.wbu.edu/eds/results?vid=0&sid=782.

Dieng, Babacar. "Reclamation in Walker's Jubilee, The Context of Development of the Historical Novel." *Journal of Pan African Studies* 2: 4 (2008):

117-127. http://search.ebscohost.com.waylandbu.idm.oclc.org/login.
aspx?direct.

Donovan, Gregory. "Several Denials and a Few Confessions: Southern Poetry
and Southern Journals." *Southern Quarterly* 45 (1): 10-18. http://search.
ebscohost.com.waylandbu.idm.oclc.org/login.aspx?direct.

Faulkner, William. "William Faulkner Banquet Speech." The Nobel Prize.
Accessed September 3, 2019. https://www.nobelprize.org/prizes/literature/
1949/faulkner/speech/.

George, Courtney. "Why and How I Teach Southern Literature, A Work in
Progress." *South, A Scholarly Journal* 50.2 (2018): 135-148. Academic
Search Complete. http://search.ebscohost.com.waylandbu.idm.oclc.org/
login.aspx?direct=true&db=a9h&AN=135571193&site=eds-live.

Kidd, Sue Monk. "Life Is a Story." YouTube video, 00:60, from Westminster
Forum February 11, 2014, posted by MySPNN, February 25, 2014.
https://www.youtube.com/watch?v=152Prmb1IK8.

MacKethan, Lucinda. "Genres of Southern Literature." *Southern Spaces* (2004).
https://www.nobelprize.org/prizes/literature/1949/faulkner/speech/.

Weathers, Glenda. "Biblical Trees, Biblical Deliverance: Literary Landscapes
of Zora Neale Hurston and Toni Morrison," *African American Review* 39
(1/2): 201. http://search.ebscohost.com.waylandbu.idm.oclc.org/login.
aspx?direct.

ONE

Postcolonialism and the Pursuit of Identity in *The Invention of Wings*

BY CINDY MCCLENAGAN

S ue Monk Kidd's novel *The Secret Life of Bees* (2002) is often characterized as not only southern fiction but also as young adult fiction—a literary work written for and about adolescents ages twelve to eighteen. Kidd's more recent novel, *The Invention of Wings* (2014), might also fall into this category, as it focuses on the lives of two adolescent females living in nineteenth-century South Carolina: abolitionist and suffragette Sarah Grimké, and her fictional African American slave, Hetty or "Handful." Although most often identified as historical fiction, *The Invention of Wings* follows these young women as they bump against timeless young-adult identity markers ranging from gender to race. Since the construction of self is a crucial part of adolescence, much of young adult literature centers on these "questions of character identity and values."[1] While E. Sybil Durand's "Forging Global Perspective through Post-colonial [sic] Young Adult Literature" does not mention Kidd's novels, it does guide educators in the selection of relevant young adult literature from the postcolonial perspective. In addition to accurate use of setting, culture, and language, Durand suggests postcolonial literature for young adults is often rooted in factual events that allow the primary theme of identity to shine.[2] Armed with Durand's and similar perspectives on adolescent development, my practical reading of *The Invention of Wings* suggests a postcolonial text focused on identity development from a cultural and adolescent perspective that provides young adult readers a space in which to pursue contemporary questions of personal growth.

Perhaps it was inevitable that postcolonialism—specifically the study of fictional texts that respond to colonization—would connect to the world of young adult literature. Both postcolonialism and young adult literature began their ascent to acceptance in the late 1970s, and both continue to resonate with scholars and readers alike. One obvious way the two intersect is in their presentation of the search for identity. After years of colonization, members of a suppressed culture often attempt to identify or redefine themselves based on both the past and the present. In part, postcolonial study considers how a culture rebuilds itself in the shadow of a dominating force. Young adult literature similarly presents teens in situations that compel active pursuit of self-construction in a world not of their making. Ultimately, both postcolonialism and young adult literature explore the growth of an identity separate from—but still within—their current environment.

As the above suggests, "one theme that postcolonial young adult literature and traditional young adult literature have in common is that of identity"—the fact of being or knowing who or what one is. Sarah Harrison notes a main characteristic of postcolonial literature is an attempt to "counteract or 'resist' the stereotypes, inaccuracies, and generalizations . . . circulated" by colonizers.[3] In counteracting these imposed stereotypes, the victims often search for and claim identities more closely aligned with their native selves. This postcolonial characteristic readily links to discussions of a theory of young adult development originated by Erik H. Erikson (1968), specifically "Identity cohesion/role confusion."[4] Erikson's adolescent stages of psychosocial development include seven specific "dimensions" or "crises" that link directly to the growth of personal identity: achievement in vocation, participation in a group, need for recognition, experimentation with roles, perspective on time, sexual identification, and commitment to an ideology.[5] Kidd's *The Invention of Wings* includes each of these individual markers in the development of an adolescent character, and thus a large portion of the novel aligns this period of personal growth with these crises to parallel and expand the postcolonial identity quest with that of the young adult's search for identity.

Although Kidd's *The Invention of Wings* demonstrates that Sarah Grimké fought tirelessly to abolish slavery and support the birth of women's rights in the mid-1800s, Grimké is not the only female character in the novel who struggles against the identity handed to her by the American culture of the early 1800s. The fictional Hetty or "Handful"—an African American slave given to the young Grimké— more strongly demonstrates the identity quest common to both postcolonial and young adult literature. By revisioning the life of a young African American slave struggling to form an identity related to her heritage while facing suppression by the dominant culture, the novel simultaneously operates as postcolonial and young adult literature. As the young Handful moves through each of Erikson's seven crises—from personal achievement in vocation to a firm commitment to an ideology—she begins to cement an identity that is at odds with early nineteenth-century southern culture.

The first "crisis" of personal identity that Erikson links to adolescent development is achievement in vocation. When first bequeathed to Sarah Grimké in *The Invention of Wings*, Handful has no idea how to pursue her new vocation as a waiting maid; she does not even know enough to open the flue before starting a fire in Sarah's bedroom.[6] She learns quickly though, and soon Handful not only masters her new trade, but also begins to learn her mother's skill—one that harkens back to her African heritage. Handful's mother (or "mauma" to Handful) is "the best seamstress in Charleston"; so good, in fact, that her owner "refuses to hire out mauma to the other ladies," suggesting she "can't have [mauma] make anything for them better than [she] make[s]" for the Grimké family.[7] Under the talented and patient eye of her mother, Handful learns the skill her mother has so carefully crafted by tying it direct-ly to their African heritage: "'This is a story quilt,' [mauma] said, and that was the first time I heard of one. [Mauma] said her mau-ma made one, and her mauma before her. All her kin in Africa, the Fon people, kept their history on a quilt."[8] By gaining achievement in two vocations—ladies' maid *and* seamstress—Handful reaches her first milestone in young adult identity development, that of mastering a vocation; however, in a more postcolonial sense she realizes her learned skills place her in a precarious position, as she and her mother now "sew too good for missus to [ever] let us go."[9]

Although initially more of a follower, Handful eventually shows qualities of leadership, the second crisis of self-development. As the novel progresses, Handful intuitively seems to understand her place not only in the local Charleston community, but also in the larger historical or African community. Handful learns of her ethnic heritage as her mother shares bits and pieces with her:

> "[When] Your granny-mauma [came from Africa; she] found
> us a spirit tree. It's just a oak tree, but she call it a Babybob like
> they have in Africa . . . Your granny-mauma wrapped the trunk
> with thread she begged and stole. She took me out there and
> say, 'We gon put our spirits in the tree so they safe from harm.'
> We kneel on her quilt from Africa, nothing but a shred now,
> and we give our spirits to the tree. She say our spirits live in the
> tree with the birds, learning to fly. She told me, 'If you leave
> this place, go get your spirit and take it with you.'"[10]

Handful later recalls this story, and actively chooses to join or par-ticipate in this heritage group: "It was all me and my idea to make us a spirit tree like [my grand-]mauma had made."[11] Much later, Handful continues to follow a strong cultural leader by joining freedom fighter Denmark Vesey in his attempt to challenge the slave-owning class of Charleston.

In the meantime, however, Handful continues the develop-ment of her identity just as Erikson suggests, with an adolescent search for recognition or affirmation from others. Handful receives recognition primarily from her mother, who not only acknowledges her growing skill as a seamstress, but also appreciates Handful's ability to write and read. At the age of fifteen, Handful's literacy leads to a higher level of individual recognition: an understanding.

> My breath hung high in my chest. *Five hundred dollars!* I marveled . . . [at] how I was worth more than every female slave they had, beside mauma. *Five hundred dollars.* . . .
> I smiled like this made [me] somebody and [then] read on to see what the rest were valued.[12]

Handful's initial thrill of pride over her value quickly turns on its head, though, as she recalls that her assigned category in the ledger falls under the label "Goods and chattel":

> We were like the gold leaf mirror and the horse saddle. Not full-fledged people. I didn't believe this, never had believed it a day in my life, but if you listen to white folks long enough, some sad, beat-down part of you starts to wonder. All that pride about what we were worth left me then. For the first time, I felt the hurt and shame of just being who I was.[13]

This sudden recognition of exactly how the dominant culture views her leads Handful to a low sense of self-worth—something temporarily detrimental to her continued identity growth.

Resuming her quest for personal and cultural identity, Handful experiments with roles outside the normal boundaries of a slave, another classic component of Erikson's psychosocial development. Handful's first non-slave endeavor occurs when Sarah teaches Handful how to read—something expressly forbidden by South Carolina law in the early 1800s.[14] However, at additional points in the text, Handful "tries on" other aspects of the life of her owners, such as enjoying a warm bath in the family's new copper bathtub. When her young mistress, Sarah Grimké, unexpectedly returns home to find Handful languidly relaxing in a bath, Sarah notes the "defiance" in Handful's eyes, a "boldness [that] seemed like more than [just] a frolic in the tub, it seemed like an act of rebellion, of usurpation."[15] Handful herself feels no need to apologize for enjoying something outside of her designated social role.

The sudden and inexplicable disappearance of her mauma gravely influences Handful's perspective on time, the fifth of the seven crises Erikson links to identity development.[16] After wrestling free from City Guards who attempt to arrest her, Handful's mauma disappears. As Handful mourns this disappearance, the past, present, and future begin to take on distinct but connected differences. In the absence of her mother, Handful first reviews each of her mother's ten story-quilt squares, and then determines to complete the quilt herself. She then draws their family heritage together as one long narrative, beginning with "the night [her] granny-mauma got sold away" from Africa, to the creation of the second spirit tree with "green leaves and a girl underneath with a book and whip coming down to strike her."[17] In determining to finish the quilt, Handful connects herself to the cultural heritage and timeline— both past and present—of her African ancestors.

Armed with a more complete understanding of time and with it, the fragility of life, Handful meets the crisis of sexual identification a bit later than adolescence. It is at the age of twenty-nine that she tells herself: "[I]f I get caught tomorrow, the Guard will kill me, and if they don't, the House will, so before I leave the earth, I might as well know what the fuss is about." The morning after this awakening, Handful's partner Goodis suggests, "'It's a fine day . . . [and] Tomorrow gon be fine, too.'"[18] Handful begrudgingly agrees, but immediately sets off to assist Denmark Vesey in his slave uprising, suggesting both her sexual identity and concept of ancestral time somehow led to the final marker of Erikson's stages, commitment to an ideology.

Handful initially commits to the ideology of life without slavery when she agrees to assist Vesey by stealing a bullet mold from the Arsenal.[19] Upon successfully completing her mission, Handful receives the recognition so often craved by adolescents and another marker of identity. She recalls "the smile on Denmark's face when I showed up and pulled a bullet mold from my basket. When I drew out the second [mold], he'd slapped his leg and said, 'You might be the best lieutenant I got.'"[20] However, her acceptance of and participation in this particular ideological approach to freedom is not without conflict, as Handful spends that night wondering, "How many people [will] those musket balls kill? . . . [On the street tomorrow] I might pass a hundred people who would die cause of me."[21] As her worldview of life without the evils of slavery grows in parallel to that of her now former mistress, Sarah Grimké, Handful determines to risk life itself by escaping from the South. After a white authority figure threatens the destruction of her mother's ancestral story quilt, Handful fully commits to the ideology of freedom. She "look[s] down at the quilt, at the slaves flying in the sky," and notes, "I hated being a slave worse than being dead. The hate I felt for [slavery] glittered so full of beauty I sank down on the floor before it." She concludes "We gonna leave here, or die trying."[22] With her identity firmly planted, Handful takes the ultimate postcolonial step of overtly rejecting the role identified for her by the dominant culture of the antebellum South. As she slips away on a steamer, Handful offers a nod to her African heritage, defiantly noting, "People say don't look back, the past is the past, but I would always look back."[23] Her escape signifies the completion of Erikson's adolescent stages of psychosocial development, resulting in Handful's commitment to an ideology and identity firmly rooted in the culture of her people.

As the adolescent Handful moved through each of Erikson's seven crises, she began to cement an identity at odds with the dominant, early nineteenth-century southern culture in which she was forced to live. Tracing Handful's growth in *The Invention of Wings* reveals how viewing identity development from both postcolonial and adolescent perspectives offers young adult readers a safe space in which to explore issues related to personal progress, despite the distance in time and space between character and native culture, and between character and reader. This search for identity—whether it be in the early 1800s of South Carolina or in a twenty-first-century country far removed from the United States—exists, especially in the lives of adolescents and persons oppressed by a culture other than their own. Rebuilding self in the shadow of any dominating force requires purposeful pursuit of self-construction, something evident in *The Invention of Wings* and many works of postcolonial and young adult literature.

The fictional modeling of characteristics of adolescent development in the context of a postcolonial-like environment offers readers two things: the realization that they control the construction of their personal identity, and the recognition that others have or likely will encounter the same identity markers despite vastly different times, spaces, and cultures. Perhaps Kidd herself sums it up best, when in an interview she responded to a question about what she hoped others would take away from *The Invention of Wings*:

> I want the reader to feel as if he or she has participated in the interior lives of the characters and felt something of their yearnings, sufferings, joys, and braveries. Empathy—taking another's experience and making it one's own—is one of the most mysterious and noble transactions a human can have.[24]

Encouraging personal identity growth that includes the consideration of others is indeed a noble human transaction, one we should not be afraid to pursue in literature or otherwise. Handful's story, that of a young African American slave struggling to form a self-identity related to her heritage despite tremendous odds, simultaneously asks both postcolonial and young adult questions, offering the opportunity for personal reflection and continued growth that extends beyond self.

NOTES

1. Thomas W., Bean and Karen Moni, "Developing Students' Critical Literacy: Exploring Identity Construction in Young Adult Fiction," *Journal of Adolescent and Adult Literacy* 46, no. 8 (May 2003): 638.
2. E. Sybil Durand, "Forging Global Perspectives through Post-Colonial Young Adult Literature," *ALAN Review*, (Winter 2013): 22, https://scholar.lib.vt.edu/ejournals/ALAN/v40n2/durand.html.
3. Sarah Harrison, "What is Postcolonial Literature?," *Teaching* The God of Small Things *in Wisconsin Great World Texts: A Program of the Center for the Humanities*, University of Wisconsin-Madison (2012), http://digitalhumanitiesseminar.ua.edu/wpcontent/uploads/2015/01/What_is_Postcolonial_Literature_.pdf.
4. Kathy H. Latrobe and Judy Drury, *Critical Approaches to Young Adult Literature* (NY: Neal-Schuman Publishers, 2009), 21.
5. Latrobe and Drury, *Critical Approaches to Young Adult Literature*, 23-24.
6. Sue Monk Kidd, *The Invention of Wings* (London: Tinder Pr., 2014), 22.
7. Kidd, *The Invention of Wings*, 4-5.
8. Kidd, *The Invention of Wings*, 97.
9. Kidd, *The Invention of Wings*, 98.
10. Kidd, *The Invention of Wings*, 53
11. Kidd, *The Invention of Wings*, 83.
12. Kidd, *The Invention of Wings*, 111.
13. Kidd, *The Invention of Wings*, 112.
14. Kidd, *The Invention of Wings*, 57, 67.
15. Kidd, *The Invention of Wings*, 114.
16. Kidd, *The Invention of Wings*, 138.
17. Kidd, *The Invention of Wings*, 147-148.
18. Kidd, *The Invention of Wings*, 242.
19. Kidd, *The Invention of Wings*, 244-245.
20. Kidd, *The Invention of Wings*, 245.
21. Kidd, *The Invention of Wings*, 246.
22. Kidd, *The Invention of Wings*, 336-337.
23. Kidd, *The Invention of Wings*, 359.
24. Sue Monk Kidd, "A Conversation with Sue Monk Kidd" (Penguin Publishing Group: 2017), http://suemonkkidd.com/books/the-invention-of-wings/reading-groups-2/.

BIBLIOGRAPHY

Bean, Thomas W., and Karen Moni. "Developing Students' Critical Literacy: Exploring Identity Construction in Young Adult Fiction." *Journal of Adolescent and Adult Literacy* 46, no. 8 (May 2003): 638-648.

Durand, E. Sybil. "Forging Global Perspectives through Post-colonial Young Adult Literature." *The ALAN Review* (Winter 2013): 21-28. https://scholar.lib.vt.edu/ejournals/ALAN/v40n2/durand.html.

Erikson, Erik. *Identity: Youth and Crisis* (1968). NY: W. W. Norton, 1994.

Harrison, Sarah. "What is Postcolonial Literature?" *Teaching* The God of Small Things *in Wisconsin Great World Texts: A Program of the Center for the Humanities,* University of Wisconsin-Madison, 2012. http://digitalhumanitiesseminar.ua.edu/wp-content/uploads/2015/01/What_is_Postcolonial_Literature_.pdf.

Kidd, Sue Monk. "A Conversation with Sue Monk Kidd." Penguin Publishing Group, 2017. http://suemonkkidd.com/books/the-invention-of-wings/reading-groups-2/.

—. *The Invention of Wings.* London: Tinder Pr., 2014.

— . *The Secret Life of Bees.* NY: Penguin Books, 2002.

Latrobe, Kathy H., and Judy Drury. *Critical Approaches to Young Adult Literature.* NY: Neal-Schuman Publishers, 2009.

Strickland, Ashley. "A Brief History of Young Adult Literature." CNN.com, April 25, 2015. http://www.cnn.com/2013/10/15/living/young-adult-fiction-evolution/index. html.

TWO

A Flying Leap of Faith:
The Invention of Wings

DEBORAH J. KUHLMANN

Sue Monk Kidd's novel *The Invention of Wings* can claim a significant place in the social discourse that often characterizes both southern and postcolonial literature. Liberation is the pivotal concern of the novel, ultimately presented as a way of being that first must be found within the individual before it can inform sound political activism. In short, freedom is spiritual first, but it requires an arduous journey to reach the place where one is willing to take a flying leap of faith. The vision in *Wings* is that freedom must progress through stages of consciousness to manifest. It is seen as a way of being that first dwells in possibility but finds power from passing through the stages of reconciliation and balance, authenticity and acceptance. Inner monologues and outer dialogues are part of each character's effort to reach full humanity, the home place of freedom, reflecting a world where neighbors inhabiting the same geographic location exist in what might as well be parallel universes that are socially, politically, and economically light-years apart.

Kidd joins our most notable southern author William Faulkner as she renders her characters via different points of view in the oscillating narratives of the two girls, Hetty and Sarah—one a slave and one the daughter of the slaveholder. These make clear that the bond they shared as children is the one that also carries them through the journey to womanhood. As well, *Wings* echoes Alice Walker's epistolary novel *The Color Purple*, where point of view is delivered in alternating chapters, composed of letters written by two sisters, Celie and Nettie. Kidd's work even shares in the tradition of Zora Neale Hurston, the master of dialect, who gives voice to the perspectives of her characters.

For example, it is no wonder why Hetty in *Invention* is headstrong and a handful, if you will. Kidd captures Hetty's own mauma's advice and support for her, as she finds realistic and believable expression in no uncertain terms: "I is a 'markable woman, and you is 'markable girl, and we ain't never gon bow and scrape to that woman."[1] And, again, when describing the quilt that is symbolic of Handful's heritage, Mauma says, "Now we putting our spirits in the tree so they safe from harm. . . ."[2] Still, even more assertive and confident and even hopeful for freedom, Kidd has Mauma declare to Hetty, "I can't buy nobody's freedom but mine and yours."[3] When Hetty investigates further as to how much it would cost for both of them, Mauma says, plain as day, "That's what you gon find out."[4] Mauma's voice—which is direct and full of self-respect and common sense and even entertaining hope, the hope of freedom— is delivered with authenticity. The reader hears her and Handful, too, throughout the book in realistic dialect, making a slave's push toward freedom and her character that would hold such a vision believable to the point that Kidd implies a needed revision of the stereotype of the slave as docile, which in no way should be considered a given or an assumption.

Like Hurston, Kidd provides a view of African American culture as one to be celebrated. Moreover, Behlor Bernice Santi in "Celebrating the Independent Spirit of Zora Neale Hurston" observes that after Alice Walker read Hurston's books for herself, she marveled at the almost perfect dialect, noting that Walker said she saw poetry, "where other writers merely saw failure to cope with English."[5] Similarly, there is nothing inadequate about Kidd's characters Handful and Mauma, whose strengths are made clear through their own voices and as such are portrayed with their full humanity intact.

Now, a healthy imagination doesn't just breed romantic idealism; it is a very necessary practical tool for survival in a world of oppression and slavery. It is an epistemological gift Hetty's (or Handful's) mother first passes on to her daughter, when she tells her from the opening sentence, "There was a time in Africa when people could fly."[6] Possibility and perspective, mystery and inquiry are evoked, a way to explore more than meets the physical eye. But Handful is no fool. She knows and tells us her "mauma was shrewd,"[7] and in the final paragraph of the introduction she confidently admits that she, too, is shrewd. Now, shrewd is a way of knowing and edgy intelligence that can decipher truth that lies somewhere between the polar opposites or contraries of a paradox. Shrewd detects and knows and gives voice to both sides. And so it is from the get-go that the reader must reckon with the intelligent edge of a girl of just ten, who in her simple inclination to embrace the world as she sees it expresses the truth of both Romanticism and idealism, while simultaneously recognizing the hard work it takes to endure and overcome, if it is possible, the reality of suffering: "Even at ten I knew this story about people flying was pure malarkey. We weren't some special people who had lost our magic. We were slave people, we weren't going anywhere. It was later I saw what she meant. We could fly alright, but wasn't any magic to it."[8]

Nevertheless, the reader is invited to explore an altered perception of reality, a mindset that defies logic, a way of being not based on circumstances. To imagine the magic of people flying evokes mystery, what H. Porter Abbott in *Real Mysteries, Narrative and the Unknowable* would call "exceeding all possibility of explanation,"[9] establishing a "capacity for wonder,"[10] embodying the unknown,[11] evoking "the need of the imagination to interpret what it sees,"[12] and rendering "the experience of unknowing."[13] As quickly as Handful moves to the gritty truth of the malarkey of such a notion, in the next breath she confirms that while there is no magic to it, at the same time it is believable. Immediately "two narrative worlds… [stand]…in the space of a single storyworld."[14] Two conflicting perceptions that sustain the paradoxical whole of parallel perspectives are the foundation upon which the structure of the entire novel rests. The worlds of Handful and Sarah in these oscillating chapters cohabit ontologically, like the simultaneous truth of magic and malarkey, and the reader must repeatedly face and entertain both. In this place or space, to remain open and allow such reconciliation of opposites is a first step toward keeping an inner balance in a world of never-ending and unfolding unpredictability. It is no easy task… this internal trek to home or self-rule.

Handful's and Sarah's lives could not be more different, but their spirits of spunk, spitfire, and solidarity bridge the gap, as they form, not without trials and tribulations, a lifelong sisterhood dedicated to the freedom to choose freedom for all. It is a labor of a lifetime for each that informs this novel with all of its intentionally induced states of bafflement.[15]

To declare there was no magic to it, to say what it was *not*, though, does not name what it *was*. Full knowledge is inaccessible, but when the incomprehensible is faced inwardly first, then the inward confrontation with the enigmatic, the oxymoronic, the contradictory, and the incongruent is actually what forges the ability to articulate it and any swift reversal of logic with the power of a trickster. Expressing such truth even just to herself sets Handful on the path to freedom, even if it is to say that something cannot be said or known. Abbott would call this kind of potential with which the reader is continually left the "art of leaving things out in such a way that they are still present."[16] A "gap," he says, is created "that not only keeps the narrative from closure but at the same time aggravates the need for closure," and thus, a "thread of curiosity and suspense…keeps the readers reading."[17] Furthermore, that "little hole in the text" that ultimately requests a "full cognitive embrace [of] the fact that there are things we simply do and cannot know"[18] invites acceptance as essential to "what it can mean to be human,"[19] creating a paradox in itself to approach understanding what cannot be understood. Likened to Keats's negative capability, "being in uncertainties, Mysteries, doubts, without any irritable reaching after fact and reason,"[20] Kidd's narrative, steeped in conundrum, both entices the curiosity and imagination of the reader and requires a high degree of tolerance for uncertainty for both the characters and the readers. Moreover, the suggestion is that accepting one's mortality with its limited knowledge, while a prerequisite for maturity and speaking one's truth with both confidence and humility, is also immensely freeing.

And yet, while unknowing invites a state of being that is open to and dwells in possibility, perhaps puzzling in *Wings* is that it also coexists with the reality of a conscience that knows right from wrong, that knows the truth is formidable and real. Sarah, as a young child, witnesses the slave woman lashed by a whip, as directed by Sarah's own mother, whom she suspected then as being "simply mean."[21] Sarah's sense of morality, like Faulkner's boy in "Barn Burning," was not so much instilled as it was intrinsic, intuitive, and immediate, with no room for doubt. With immense clarity she stares "transfixed as the back of [the slave woman's dress] spouts blood, blooms of red that open like petals. I cannot reconcile the savagery of the blows with the mellifluous way she keens or the beauty of the roses coiling the trellis of her spine."[22] It is crystal clear from Kidd that within the human dwells a crystal-clear conscience, and it stands as the springboard to launch liberation, being fundamental to voicing one's individual, original, and therefore authentic perception.

This event was pivotal in shaping Sarah, but her sense of self comes early in her young life and, she says, out of her destiny.[23] Her sense of purpose, without any doubt or uncertainty, to be a female lawyer at a time where there were none she attributes to a spiritual seed planted within her by God.[24] That said, her knowing and seeing is all but a cross for her to bear. She even laments her loneliness as a young girl in a world of corruption where her own ideas are completely alien, like those of Huck Finn, and antithetical to the mainstream of so-called civilization. We can, if we are willing, choose what is humane and serves our humanity and that of others if we will listen to the inner light that is within us, according to Kidd. It will light the way to both independence and interdependence. But, for Sarah, it requires sacrifice.

What exacerbates Sarah's loneliness is the irony of knowing but being powerless to speak, at first from shock and later from fear. In short, Sarah remained mute for a week and ultimately developed a stutter or stammer that lasted for years. One very prominent step in her venture to personhood was the day she was moved from the nursery. By this time in her young life she had seen the unspeakable horror of the torture of Handful's mother, and she finds she is unable to answer when her mother simply asks whether her new surroundings are to her liking. "The door slammed in my throat, and the silence hung there."[25] Her search for her own voice in spite of knowing all that she does about herself and her world will become a lifelong endeavor and a thread toward freedom throughout the novel. Nor is it surprising that Kidd's view in *The Dance of the Dissident Daughter* seems embodied by Sarah here, as she wrote, "And it came to me all of a sudden that becoming empowered as a woman required three similar things: a soul of one's own, the ability or means to voice it, and finally, the courage to voice it at all."[26] That vision of empowerment in *Wings*, though, is not magic. That would be pure malarkey in this world where women's assertions counted for pretty much nothing. The path to fulfillment in Kidd's novel is the striving for integrity, when women, slave and slaveholder alike, were not afforded that value or privilege. The toil, the work was to move toward the autonomy of being able to proclaim "the truth and nothing but the truth," even when that meant—as Ursula Le Guin noted—"when women speak truly, they speak subversively,"[27] making them politically dangerous and always at risk.

Is it any wonder then that young Sarah decides to teach Handful to read and write? By allowing it, however, Handful was at risk of her very life. Nevertheless, Handful, like Sarah, is shrewd. They both navigate a sea of troubles courageously, without any arms to take up. Instead, for both, the road to freedom is internal first, captured in Sarah's gritty realization in her own mind that "At age eleven I owned a slave I couldn't free."[28] With full awareness of her own innocence ripped away, cruel ironies abound for Sarah and Handful alike. Sarah has her own kind of shrewdness that begins when she contributes to the development of Handful's intellectual if not physical freedom, even if it was against the law. And yet theirs is a complicated friendship, to say the least. For both girls to connect with one another, to choose love and friendship above the whole world that would reject them, signifies the choice early on to honor their own experience. It is the firm footing that will carry them toward the hope of emancipation.

This first step toward an emotional bond took immense courage for Handful, but it was the beginning of a transformative journey to listen to her own heart always, as did Sarah—a quality that would serve them throughout their lifetimes:

> [She] put her arms around me. It was hard to know where
> things stood. People say love gets fouled up by a difference big
> as ours. I didn't know for sure whether Miss Sarah's feelings
> came from love or guilt. I didn't know whether mine came
> from love or a need to be safe. She loved me and pitied me.
> And I loved and used her. It never was a simple thing.[29]

Again, clarity and insight are sharp and definitive, and at the same time what is "never simple" is left to the reader's imagination, a mystery, an "opening in the text" that Abbott would call the "art of leaving things out in such a way that they are still present,"[30] a "gap that not only keeps the narrative from closure but at the same time aggravates the need for closure,"[31] "creating the thread of curiosity and suspense that keeps readers reading."[32] Will these girls be able to find their way to self-sovereignty in this world of injustice and oppression and forbidden freedom? How does anyone? Sue Monk Kidd gives us a vision for just that aspiration, and it is the eagerness to follow the deepest desires of one's own heart that is the compass to follow.

Sarah ultimately relinquishes her dream to be a lawyer and chooses the spiritual path of being a Quaker, and a minister at that.

She falls deeply in love with Quaker Israel Morris but chooses not to marry him, for she understood she could not have both him and herself. "I'd chosen the regret I could live with best, that's all. I'd chosen the life I belonged to."[33] Just as she had done as a child and just as she had done before her romance with Israel began, she followed her true north or what she learned the Quakers called the Inner Voice, the one to which she listened in spite of all the other voices telling her otherwise, for, as she says, it was "dense with God"[34] to "Go north."[35] It is this exactly that will eventually allow her to champion her own voice, clear and strong, that she would use to stand as an abolitionist against slavery, this daughter of "a Southern patriot, a slaveholder, an aristocrat."[36] Her realization had been prompted, too, by Handful saying to her that her "*body might be a slave, but not my mind. For you it's the other way around.*"[37] Sarah recognized then it was her "mind [that] had been shackled."[38]

To listen not to the pronouncements of others but to her own inward view was what catapulted her to wholeness, maturity, and her own full humanity and full acceptance at middle age after speaking to the Anti-Slavery Society, "*I'm who I am.*"[39] This authority that comes to her consciousness emerges from her moral center, deep within her own person, and exercising it is necessary for deliverance. When she does, her stammering finally leaves. To a great degree the most poignant query of the entire novel rests with Sarah's resonating question to herself: "How does one know the voice is God's? I believed the voice bidding me to go north belonged to him, though perhaps what I really heard that day was my own impulse to freedom. Perhaps it was my own voice. [Did] it matter?"[40] Her rhetorical question leaves a "gap." No answer. No certainty. But mystery for which both characters and readers must make intellectual room.

Handful, too, chooses to leave the man she loves to embrace her release from the patriarchy that has enslaved her body. Handful in a hundred ways never doubts what she sees, and in so doing embraces what she knows, even if she must remain silent as well, during all of her slave life. However, like her mother before her, who tells her story in code in the images of a quilt, she is skilled in outfoxing the fox. She admits to herself as she and Sarah, in disguise, risk everything to travel north for their freedom: "I saw it then, the strange thing between us. *Not love, is it?*"[41] They make good use of the veil that would hide their faces, ironically and traditionally dressed for mourning, to carry them to the place where they can be open with their faces, their views, and their lives; to secure, as Kidd describes in *Dissident Daughter*, "a soul of one's own, the ability or means to voice it, and the courage to voice it at all."[42] As the ship pulls out of Charleston harbor, Handful hears "the blackbird wings" just like the ones on her mother's quilt, the ones she described when she told her "There was a time in Africa the people could fly . . . they flew like blackbirds."[43] Kidd in *Daughter* calls this the "inner authority *as a woman* . . . [as they experience] the abiding strength, resilience, potency, and substance that comes when a woman dwells in the solid center of herself."[44] The novel ends in this experience as they take off and fly to a new life, new possibilities. All that said, there is no certainty in this, no absence of sacrifice or risk. It is a flying leap of faith into the unknown, into the next chapter, even the next moment of their lives.

As Abbott describes it, even the conclusion keeps "the reader delightedly immersed in the mystery of their coming into being,"[45] not unlike Kidd's insight in *Daughter*, when she identifies such a moment as [that] which "is our home."[46] It is coming to an acceptance of *what is*, both what is and what is not known or seen, where empowerment and being fully reside. To leap into the being of one's life is Kidd's paradigm for liberation. As she says in *Daughter*, "[To] . . . accept where we are standing in the river now, and . . . enter the immediacy of it, even when it's painful, because by doing so we are being present to our lives . . . We may not realize it, but [it is] by being present and looking deeply, we are becoming activists."[47] We are becoming ourselves, forever being in a moment of becoming. It is on that same note *The Invention of Wings* ends, of course, in a poetic image that can render the reality of such a mystery: "We rode onto the shining water, onto the far distance,"[48] signifying a world where wings not only can be but are invented, and where freedom is chosen in sparkling moments of faith.

NOTES

1. Sue Monk Kidd, *The Invention of Wings*, *(New York: Viking, 2014), 76.*

2. Kidd, *The Invention of Wings*, 83.

3. Kidd, *The Invention of Wings*,100.

4. Kidd, *The Invention of Wings*,100.

5. Behlor Bernice Santi, "Celebrating the Independent Spirit of Zora Neale Hurston," Writer (*Kalmbach Publishing Co.*) 124, no. 2 (February 2011): 8–9, http://search.ebscohost.com.waylandbu.idm.oclc.org/login.aspx? direct=true&db=a9h&AN=57270558&site=eds-live.

6. Kidd, *The Invention of Wings*, 3.

7. Kidd, *The Invention of Wings*, 3.

8. Kidd, *The Invention of Wings*, 3.

9. H. Porter Abbott, *Real Mysteries, Narrative and the Unknowable* (Columbus: The Ohio State University Press, 2013), 50.

10. Abbott, *Real Mysteries*, 48.

11. Abbott, *Real Mysteries*, 49.

12. Abbott, *Real Mysteries*, 49.

13. Abbott, *Real Mysteries*, 22.

14. Abbott, *Real Mysteries*, 99.

15. Abbott, *Real Mysteries*, 9.

16. Abbott, *Real Mysteries*, 110.

17. Abbott, *Real Mysteries*, 112.

18. Abbott, *Real Mysteries*, 115.

19. Abbott, *Real Mysteries*, 114.

20. John Keats, "Letter to George and Thomas Keats," in *The Norton Anthology of English Literature*, vol. D. 9th ed., ed. Stephen Greenblatt (New York: Norton, 2012), 968.

21. Kidd, *The Invention of Wings*, 9.

22. Kidd, *The Invention of Wings*, 10-11.

23. Kidd, *The Invention of Wings*, 20.

24. Kidd, *The Invention of Wings*, 21.

25. Kidd, *The Invention of Wings*, 12.

26. Sue Monk Kidd, *The Dance of the Dissident Daughter* (San Francisco: Harper Collins, 200), 198.

27. Kidd, *The Dance of the Dissident Daughter,* 205.
28. Kidd, *The Invention of Wings,* 15.
29. Kidd, *The Invention of Wings,* 54.
30. Abbott, *Real Mysteries,*110.
31. Abbott, *Real Mysteries,* 112.
32. Abbott, *Real Mysteries,* 112.
33. Kidd, *The Invention of Wings, 295.*
34. Kidd, *The Invention of Wings, 210.*
35. Kidd, *The Invention of Wings, 209.*
36. Kidd, *The Invention of Wings, 298.*
37. Kidd, *The Invention of Wings, 210.*
38. Kidd, *The Invention of Wings, 210.*
39. Kidd, *The Invention of Wings, 327.*
40. Kidd, *The Invention of Wings, 210.*
41. Kidd, *The Invention of Wings, 355.*
42. Kidd, *The Dance of the Dissident Daughter, 198.*
43. Kidd, *The Invention of Wings, 3.*
44. Kidd, *The Dance of the Dissident Daughter, 197.*
45. Abbott, *Real Mysteries,* 56.
46. Kidd, *The Dance of the Dissident Daughter, 220.*
47. Kidd, *The Dance of the Dissident Daughter,* 221.
48. Kidd, *The Invention of Wings, 359.*

BIBLIOGRAPHY

Abbott, H. Porter. *Real Mysteries, Narrative and the Unknowable.* Columbus: The Ohio State University Press, 2013.

Keats, John. 2012. "Letter to George and Thomas Keats." In *The Norton Anthology of English Literature.* Vol. D. 9th ed., Edited by Stephen Greenblatt, 967-986. New York: Norton.

Kidd, Sue Monk. *The Dance of the Dissident Daughter.* San Francisco: Harper Collins, 2002.

Kidd, Sue Monk. *The Invention of Wings.* New York: Viking, 2014.

Santi, Behlor Bernice. "Celebrating the Independent Spirit of Zora Neale Hurston." *Writer (Kalmbach Publishing Co.)* 124, no. 2 (February 2011): 8–9. http://search.ebscohost.com.waylandbu.idm.oclc.org/login.aspx?direct=true&db=a9h&AN=57270558&site=eds-live.

THREE

She May Bee Like Jesus: African American Female Christ Figure in *The Secret Life of Bees*

ERIN HEATH

Representations of mental disorder in Hollywood cinema commonly present figures who are dangerous, pitiable, or both.[1] Frequently shown as criminal masterminds or psychotic killers, people with mental disorders have long been portrayed in ways that are neither enviable nor admirable. The alternative examples usually appear as pathetic figures that exist to demonstrate the benevolence of their cognitively typical caretakers. *The Secret Life of Bees* subverts this common narrative by celebrating its non-neurotypical character's voice and sacrifice by establishing her as a Christ figure.

Based on Sue Monk Kidd's book of the same name, the 2008 film *The Secret Life of Bees* directed by Gina Prince-Bythewood includes religious iconography that presents a consistently black female-centered approach to Christianity. While the relationships in this film operate on a literal level, loving and supporting Lily Owen's search for a mother, they also provide a figurative retelling of the Christ story, told with a mostly black female cast and with a primary character who appears to be cognitively atypical. The one significant white character, Lily, serves as an audience surrogate and a representative of contemporary Christians. Making the sole white character the "everyman" figure who explores the "otherness" of the non-white characters is a trope that reinforces white privilege, but the text uses a female child, which helps reduce or limit much of the racial condescension present in, for example, much white savior fiction. And the narrative does not make the white character the savior: instead she is saved by the nonwhite women. The African American beekeepers, August Boatwright (Queen Latifah) and May Boatwright (Sophie Okonedo) operate as representations of Mary and Jesus. I argue that in an interesting twist on traditionally white male-dominated normate or neurotypical narratives in American Christianity, May Boatwright, an African American woman with a probable mental disorder, serves as the Christ figure. This feminized non-neurotypical African American Christian narrative brings to the forefront a significant message of inclusivity, acceptance, and empathy in the Christ story.

The Secret Life of Bees tells the story of a young white girl in South Carolina searching for the history of her mother while escaping from an abusive father. Lily Owens runs away with her nanny Rosaleen Daise, played by Jennifer Hudson. The pair travel to a town written on the back of one of her mother's meager possessions. When they arrive in Tiburon, South Carolina, they stay with three African American beekeepers. The three sisters, August, June (Alicia Keys), and May, employ Lily and Rosaleen as Lily tries to uncover the truth about her mother and find love.

The film begins its depictions of a black female-centered Christianity with Lily's picture of a black Virgin Mary. Lily finds this picture in a box of items owned by her mother, leading her to cherish it. American Christianity has a propensity for representations of Jesus and Mary that appear based on Western European iconography. Despite Jesus and Mary's being Middle Eastern Jews, Western European art frequently depicts him and his mother as fair-skinned Caucasians. In her article "'Our Father, God; Our Brother, Christ; or are We Bastard Kin?': Images of Christ in African American Painting," Kymberly Pinder asserts that

fashioning a Christ in one's own image is not a new phenomenon in art or religious history. Just as Chinese and Indian artists
make the facial features of the Buddha similar to those of their
people, Ethiopians and other Christians of color have been
making dark-skinned Christs and saints for centuries.[2]

Pinder goes on to discuss the importance of depictions of black
religious figures in African American culture as resisting the white
Eurocentric culture: "The motif of the suffering Christ in their
paintings engages issues of African American cultural identity
which were relevant then and still are today."[3] Pinder argues that
these images served as a form of resistance and reclaim the Christ
narrative for their pwn culture. This reclaiming of Mary becomes
important to the Boatwright sisters and ultimately Lily as they connect and identify with the black Virgin Mary.

The black Mary in *The Secret Life of Bees* that Lily repeatedly
encounters operates as an object of discussion and a point of rebellion by the sisters against a white male Eurocentric Christian worldview. Lily even asks the sisters "Why do you put a Negro Mary on
your honey?" to which June replies "You mean why is she black or
why is she on the honey?" June sees Lily's question as a challenge
against their presentation of Mary as black. By printing and shar-
ing the image of a black Mary on their honey, they reclaim Mary
as their own, remaking her in their image, and probably creating a
more historically accurate image. Lily's question encourages August
to tell the story of their black Mary statue and how she became the
center of their small church. By focusing on Mary and representing
her as black, the sisters control the narrative of Christianity and
take back the power of her representation.

The film introduces the audience and Lily to the church created by August and her sisters as a markedly feminine African
American denomination, with Mary as a central figure. A group
of African American women gathers in the family's living room as
June plays the cello. August, the clear leader of the group, provides
the sermon about the discovery of the black wooden Mary figure.

August stands before them and tells them that she will tell "The story of our Mary."[4] Mary is not just *a* woman but *their* woman. This wooden figure becomes their personification of the mother of God, and it is a black woman like them. In Catherine B. Emanuel's article "The Archetypal Mother: The Black Madonna in Sue Monk Kidd's *The Secret Life of Bees*," she asserts that "Blacks then in America have had a complex relationship with the church whose ideology and texts on the one hand served to oppress them and on the other provided some comfort and solace, but only in a re-writing from white ideology."[5] August's cadence and her tone echo the authority of southern African American preachers leading their congregations. August operates as the authority figure and tells the group that "Mary was strong, constant, and had a mother's heart," as she taps her own breast, again emphasizing their personal intimate connection to their faith, their femininity, and their strength. August's words reverberate as each of the women go to the wooden Mary statue and touch a red heart painted on her chest. This church serves as the center of their religious expression. With a female leader and an emphasis on a Mary rather than Jesus, the film presents an intimate and empathetic feminine side of Christian fellowship.

While Lily serves as the lead in the story, around which the story is told, she also operates as the audience surrogate examining the lives of these interesting sisters and seeking absolution for her sin. As part of the more figurative expression of this Christ story, she becomes a representative of mankind or more pointedly of womankind. Catherine B. Emanuel discusses the way that "Lily welcomes a religion that embraces her, that feeds her, that provides a woman's face."[6] As the everywoman character, Lily spends most of the film looking for forgiveness for accidentally murdering her mother at the age of four. The murder of her mother defines how Lily thinks about herself. Her first words in the film reveal this: "I killed my mother when I was four years old. That's what I knew about myself." As if that is the only thing that she is certain about in her life. Her "original sin" shapes how she sees herself and serves as a mirror to Eve. It is from there that she progresses through the film on a journey to salvation and redemption. She embodies the Christian woman in need of redemption and forgiveness in a very Christian worldview that sees everyone as seeking redemption and forgiveness through Jesus Christ's life and sacrifice.

Soon after May's tragic suicide, Lily comes crying to August looking for answers. She tells August that "I don't mean to be a bad person, but I just can't help it." She sees herself as full of sin and asks August for forgiveness. August becomes like Mary, a conduit for Lily's absolution. Only after May has died and sacrificed herself in a Christ-like fashion can Lily ask for forgiveness and receive it. The last lines in the film include "I have to wake up and forgive again."[7] The film shows forgiveness as more than a single act but a process that acknowledges the ongoing struggle of human imperfection and divine absolution. The film provides these lines with uplifting images of Lily living happily around the women who have become her family. Lily becomes all Christians who ask for absolution from their sins. The film shows her finding absolution continually in her happy ending, not because she is a bad person, but because of her imperfect humanity and God's continual forgiveness. The importance of forgiving one's self and the ongoing process of grace serves as the film's central message.

As Lily serves as a surrogate for Christian women, August operates as the embodiment of the Virgin Mary. August's parallels are often visual, as she frequently wears blue, a common visual indicator of the Virgin Mary in Western European art. Even in an all-white outfit to interact with the bees, she has a blue scarf around her neck. This visual marker of the Virgin Mary appears throughout August's representation, and the film bolsters this when she asserts that it is her favorite color. She also stands next to the wooden Mary in the same pose with her fist forward. During her sermon about finding the wooden Mary, August does more than face Mary but also stands beside her in solidarity with the beloved statue. August's maternal wisdom provides grounding and strength that the other characters orbit around, similar to the way that their religion focuses on Mary.

Her maternal relationship to May similarly strengthens August's position as the mother of Christ.

The character of May is a somewhat unexpected Christ figure, as she is an African American woman with a mental disorder. I use the term mental disorder, as it is a broad term used in the *Diagnostic and Statistical Manual of Mental Disorder* for many varied non-neurotypical experiences. The audience's introduction to May is as she stands behind her protective sister June, but as Lily and Rosaleen enter the parlor, May moves to sit under the protective arm of the Virgin Mary statue. Like a child at the foot of her mother, May leans towards the wooden Mary and gazes at the new guests. May's proximity to Mary continues in the scene of the family's church service. While the other women reverently touch Mary's painted heart, May hugs Mary like a child might hug her mother. The gesture appears very personal and uninhibited. Her physical position as childlike beside the maternal wooden Mary establishes her characterization as the child of the Virgin Mary.

The film demonstrates ways that May's childlike affect arises from her great love and empathy. Whenever May encounters something that she perceives as sad or evil, she cries. She cries at the mention of her dead sister, the sight of Rosaleen's scar, and several other moments in the film. While initially presented negatively, her extreme empathy evolves into something profound and valuable. This level of significant empathy leads Lily to ask August, "She's a little different, huh?" and "She sure gets upset easy."[8] Lily's questions imply that she wants to know if May might have a diagnosed mental disorder. August replies that "The doctors kept telling us to put her away."[9] Her response affirms that medical professionals understand May to have a mental disorder that should result in her institutionalization. Rather than dwelling on this understanding of May's mental disorder, the film moves the focus to a more religious or spiritual way of considering May's experience. August explains that when May goes out to the wall in the backyard it serves as "The Wailing Wall, like the one in Jerusalem. The Jewish people go there to mourn. See, they write their prayers on tiny pieces of paper, and they tuck 'em in the wall. And that's what Miss May does. Those bits of paper are all the heavy feelings May carries around."[10] May's great empathy and her connection to Judaism through her performance of grief serves as a strong indicator of her Christ-like qualities. She feels compassion and love for everyone, especially for those who suffer or are in need. Her Jewish-inspired wall helps her absorb and manage her burdensome emotion and empathy.

May continues in her similarities to Jesus with her allusions to her premature death. While talking about May's great empathy, Lily speaks of it in admiration. "Miss May, I know you get real sad sometimes. My Daddy never feels. He never felt anything. I had rather be like you."[11] While May's intense emotional responses to the suffering of others initially appear in the film as a weakness, eventually Lily discusses it as a point of admiration. May responds that "A worker bee weigh less than a flower petal, but she can fly with a load heavier than her, but she only lives four or five weeks. Sometimes not feelin' is the only way you can survive."[12] May relates her own troubling experience to the short-lived venerable bees who have great strength and carry great burdens. Because the bees carry such great weight, they cannot endure their difficult lives for long, as May cannot endure her burdens.

The song she repeats likewise foreshadows her premature death: "Place a beehive on my grave and let the honey soak through. When I'm dead and gone, that's what I want from you."[13] While a sweet dirge, it establishes her interest in and fixation on death. Jesus told his disciples on several occasions that they should expect him to die and be resurrected. Two of those examples include the passage in Mathew 16:21-28. It states that Jesus "began to show his disciples that he must go to Jerusalem and suffer many things from the elders and chief priests and scribes, and be killed. . . ." Similarly in Mathew 17:22–23, the passage reads "The Son of Man is going to be betrayed into the hands of men. They will kill him, and after three days he will rise." Like Jesus, May makes clear that her life will end prematurely as part of an act of love.

The rest of May's dirge adds further parallels to the Christ tale. It provides a wish for May to remain on earth with her loved ones even after death.

> Place a beehive on my grave
> let the honey soak through.
> I'm dead and gone,
> what I want from you.
> streets of heaven are gold and sunny,
> I'll stick with my plot and a pot of honey.
> a beehive on my grave
> let the honey soak through.[14]

May asserts that she will remain on earth after her death in that she will "stick with my plot and a pot of honey."[15] In using a metaphor throughout the film that bees are like people and honey their love, May wants to remain with the people on earth and asserts that the honey or love will be with her there. While Jesus did die as he foreshadowed, a tenant of the Christian faith is the belief that he returned and exists with people on earth.

May's very life echoes visually and thematically some meaningful elements in Jesus's story, especially those that might be considered more feminine. Lily finds May crouched on the ground luring a roach out of her home with crumbs and marshmallows. While T. Ray calls the act ridiculous, when Lily sees May do this it reminds her of her mother. It also speaks to an extreme love and adoration for all of God's creatures.

The film also shows May braiding the hair of her sisters and Lily. By braiding hair, May serves the women around her. The affectionate and caring act takes time and demonstrates love in a physical and intimate way, as Jesus did when he washed the feet of his disciples (John 13:1-17). Both physical acts of grooming illustrate love through non-sexualized physical contact. Compassion and affection continually serve as the center of both figures' narratives.

Another parallel includes a scene where May plays in the sprinklers with Rosaleen. The two women seem to be playing in the water and it sparkles at their feet as they dance and laugh. The light and the angle of the shot provide a momentary impression that they are standing on the water. The film's suggestion that May appears to dance on water creates one more visual connection to Christ.

May's death, more than any element of her character, echoes the sacrifice of Jesus. While May's death appears as a suicide straightforwardly, Jesus knew that he would soon be killed in Jerusalem, and yet he did not run away from his fate. "Behold, we are going up to Jerusalem, and the Son of Man will be betrayed to the chief priests and to the scribes; and they will condemn Him to death and deliver Him to the Gentiles; and they will mock Him, and scourge Him, and spit on Him, and kill Him. And the third day He will rise again" (Mark 10:33-34).

Despite May's act being a suicide rather than capital punishment, she kills herself as a sacrifice to help those around her. In her letter to her sisters, she writes "I'm tired of carrying around the weight of the world. I'm just going to lay it down now. It's my time to die and it's your time to live. Don't mess it up. Love, May."[16] As Jesus carried the burdens of mankind and gave himself to relieve the world of sin, May sees that she must sacrifice herself so that her sisters can move on. She sees herself, much like the worker bees, as carrying a great burden of evil and sadness in the world. She must let these burdens down so that others may forgive and be forgiven.

The film presents May's death with visual similarities to the crucifixion. The first visual indicator comes as August finds May's dead body in the shallow river. A large rock, like the ones in the wailing wall, holds May's body underwater, a literal burden in death that represents the emotional burdens she carried in life. The rock rests on her chest, while her arms spread out like Jesus's arms on the cross. The film shows her death in this significant pose, and immediately follows it with a shot showing August pulling May from the water. August leans against the river bank and holds May's body in her lap. She cries in anguish as June leans over them and also mourns. August's posture in cradling the dead May in her lap resembles closely the many paintings of Mary cradling Jesus after the crucifixion. This *pieta* serves as an important moment in the film, as it provides both a tragic turning point and reenacts an important moment in Mary's story. The biblical imagery places emphasis on Mary's life and the importance of the story of Jesus. These similarities correlate with the rest of the film's focus on the feminine aspects of Christianity.

Upon May's death, there remains no *impediment* to June and August moving on. June can finally get married because of May's sacrifice. While May asserted that June was not getting married because she was afraid, June denied this. August similarly said that she would have gotten married, but "loved [her] freedom more."[17] While never overtly stated in the film, neither woman would leave May to get married. More overtly, August describes a fight between June and her boyfriend Neil (Nate Parker): "Some people rather die than forgive and June is one of them."[18] It is only with May's death that June finds forgiveness enough to call Neil back to accept his marriage proposal. May tells her sisters in her suicide note to not waste their lives, and June makes an effort by forgiving Neil. May's sacrifice allows June to forgive, in a small way that echoes Jesus's sacrifice so that the world might be forgiven for their sins.

May Boatwright is a remarkable character in her presence in American film. She appears as an African American woman with a mental disorder who is neither a prop nor a victim. Instead, she serves as a cogent, caring, affectionate woman who loves and is loved by her sisters. While she feels too much, she does so in a way that appears admirable in the film. May's empathy is venerable, if tragic. She, like Jesus, dies for love. Their parallels provide a meaningful lesson in an inclusive narrative about sacrifice and forgiveness. The film as directed by Gina Prince-Bythewood embraces May's similarities to Christ in Kidd's book and furthers the comparison in a beautiful celebration of a humble, empathetic character.

NOTES

1. Patricia A. Stout, Jorge Villegas, and Nancy A. Jennings, "Images of Mental Illness in the Media: Identifying Gaps in the Research," *Schizophrenia Bulletin* 30, (January 1, 2004): 543-561.

2. Kymberly Pinder, "'Our Father, God; Our Brother, Christ; or are we bastard kin?': Images of Christ in African American Painting," *African American Review* 31, no. 2 (1997): 223-233.

3. Pinder, "Our Father, God."

4. *The Secret Life of Bees,* DVD, directed by Gina Prince-Bythewood, performed by Dakota Fanning, Queen Latifah, Jennifer Hudson, Alicia Keys, and Sophie Okonedo (2008; Century City, California: Fox Searchlight Pictures).

5. Catherine B. Emanuel, "The Archetypal Mother: The Black Madonna in Sue Monk Kidd's *The Secret Life of Bees,*" *West Virginia University Philological Papers* (2005): 120.

6. Emanuel, "The Archetypal Mother," 119.

7. *The Secret Life of Bees,* DVD.

8. *Bees,* DVD.

9. *Bees,* DVD.

10. *Bees,* DVD.

11. *Bees,* DVD.

12. *Bees,* DVD.

13. *Bees,* DVD.

14. *Bees,* DVD.

15. *Bees,* DVD.

16. *Bees,* DVD.

17. *Bees,* DVD.

18. *Bees,* DVD.

BIBLIOGRAPHY

Emanuel, Catherine B. 2005. "The Archetypal Mother: The Black Madonna in Sue Monk Kidd's *The Secret Life of Bees.*" *West Virginia University Philological Papers* 115.

Pinder, Kymberly N.1. 1997. "'Our Father, God; Our Brother, Christ; or are we bastard kin?': Images of Christ in African American Painting." *African American Review* 31, no. 2: 223-233.

Secret Life of Bees, The. Film directed by Gina Prince-Bythewood, Performed by Dakota Fanning, Queen Latifah, Jennifer Hudson, Alicia Keys, and Sophie Okonedo. 2008. Century City, California: Fox Searchlight Pictures, 2015. DVD.

Stout, Patricia A., Jorge Villegas, and Nancy A. Jennings. "Images of Mental Illness in the Media: Identifying Gaps in the Research." *Schizophrenia Bulletin* 30, (January 1, 2004): 543-561. *ScienceDirect*, EBSCO*host* (accessed August 29, 2016).

FOUR

Secrets of Being in
The Secret Life of Bees

DEBORAH J. KUHLMANN

I f *The Invention of Wings* delivers a profound vision of freedom, Sue Monk Kidd's earlier and most well-known novel *The Secret Life of Bees* tackles an even greater mystery, and that is a view of love as a sacred space in the heart where liberty, in fact, resides. *The Secret Life of Bees* could as well have been titled *The Secrets of Being*, as Kidd renders the transformational stages of the coming of age of Lily Owens, but they stand also as the metaphorical stages required to cross the psychological, spiritual, and theological terrain any pilgrim in pursuit of full humanity or seeker of holy places must travel.

Essential mysteries, as the title implies, are the primary concern of *The Secret Life of Bees.* Worldly or secular identity—that is, social-economic-political identity—is not. The mission for this band of characters, all of whom must reject any identity thrust upon them by the social and segregated norms of the time if they are to "*not mess up* [their] *time to live*,"[1] is to take their birthright as human beings to define and even redefine who they are in a spiritual rather than a material light. In "The Archetypal Mother: The Black Madonna in Sue Monk Kidd's *The Secret Life of Bees*,"

Catherine Emanuel notes that Lily's search, which begins as a quest for a psychological identity, expands to archetypal dimensions.[2] All must take the road less traveled: the black women, led by their older sister August, a land-owning, atypical woman for the times; the adolescent and motherless white girl Lily, who has only her wits to help her survive her brutal and damaged, economically disadvantaged father; and Rosaleen, full of soul, but trapped, like all the others, in this racist, sexist patriarchy that would try to imprison them in a conformist identity.

Further stations on this most difficult pilgrimage include enduring loss, finding courage, seeking redemption, forging bonds, voicing truth, making space for contradictions, fostering forgiveness, taking ownership and responsibility for self, embracing hope amid ambiguity, and relentlessly persisting in love.[3] This path leads to a way of being free of the trappings of this world, but it also celebrates the crux of one's humanity and the experience of vulnerability in it, for it is exactly in this vulnerability that one can experience the need for and so then respond with empathy for another. Actually, Kidd herself even declared in "Life Is A Story," a lecture given at the Westminster Forum, that empathy is the felt experience she would want her readers to have,[4] clearly a pivotal value and even a mystery of the heart and imagination that is central to all of her works. Charles Mathewes, Carolyn M. Barbour Professor of Religious Studies at the University of Virginia, has published two major books on St. Augustine and delivered a lecture series for The Great Courses Plus on Augustine's *The City of God*. Mathewes expresses St. Augustine's vision in *The City of God* in "Sacrifice and Ritual," a lecture on Book 10 of that work, where Augustine submits that while we are always in the world, we should not flee our humanity but embrace it, understanding that we are, in fact, human *so that* we might choose to know that which is sacred and go to our neighbor in compassion.[5] Kidd's vision echoes this. Indeed, August even tells Lily, "The whole problem with people is . . . they know what matters, but they don't choose it . . . Lifting a person's heart—now, *that* matters."[6] But then August delivers an even more blunt and inescapably unambiguous blow of reality in her firm but tender queenly way: "The hardest thing on earth is choosing what matters."[7] It is not the easy way at all, even a steep climb at times, but no matter the circumstances, it can be chosen. And Lily does.

Still, an open mindset, one that can make room for polarities and paradoxes, possibilities and probabilities amid ultimate uncertainty or a cloud of not-knowing, is required. This gets right at Kidd's ontological perspective on what it means to be human, and its rendering in *Bees* compels receptiveness of the character but also of the reader with the same kind of approach to being. H. Porter Abbott in *Real Mysteries, Narrative and the Unknowable* describes that would be open to the coexistence of two opposed frames of mind at once.[8] This worldview is observed by Judith Hebb in "Religious Imagery in The *Secret Life of Bees* and *The Mermaid Chair*," when she states that the Masthead Mary and Our Lady of Chains "represent both oppression as well as freedom,"[9] so that readers must reckon with characters who are burdened with all manner of the suffering that may beset the human condition but can still find freedom in the choice to love. Like Lily, who is actually jolted into a new way of thinking,[10] so goes the possibility for the reader. And so goes another secret of being in *The Secret Life of Bees*.

The choice to love that informs Kidd's work, as chronicled in *The Dance of the Dissident Daughter, A Woman's Journey from Christian Tradition to the Sacred Feminine*, is rooted in Christianity. As she says, "I see myself in the Christian tradition, but I also call myself an orthodox eclectic. I explore different avenues to transcendence."[11] In *The City of God*, St. Augustine asserts that humans need to worship,[12] according to Mathewes in "Splendid Vices and Happiness in Hope (Book 5)," a lecture on the classically Christian text. In this sense an Augustinian view is affirmed and kin to the one in *The Secret Life of Bees*, as these women in this novel create rituals to glorify Mary, mother of Jesus, clearly longing for devotion to a deity, even though they are not Christian and could be considered pagan or self-invented or post-Christian at best. Nevertheless, this seeming assimilation of spiritual practice, which they invent, finds expression at a kind of theological crossroads on this path to discovering that the choice to love is always right at hand.

For Lily the traction needed to move forward can only be gained when love and acceptance of life and self is first nurtured and mothered, as August does for Lily in the absence of Lily's own biological mother, until it secures a permanent home in her individual psyche. Certainly, the maternal is primary here and comes first. Still, this particular focus on the mother rather than on the Christ could be considered a reversal of Christianity that nevertheless holds within it a coexistence or paradox that is both essentially Christian and feminine, an integration or convergence or even amalgamation of both. Regardless, it is most principally a sacred lane to love, to Christ-consciousness, if you will, by letting go of the small self and opening to the larger mystery of Being to which Lily is invited, well rooted in the paradox that it is in losing one's life or in letting it go to something greater, that love is found.

Loss is, in fact, central to the entire narrative, told from the fresh point of view of an innocent, yet one who, not unlike Huckleberry Finn or Jane Eyre to whom Kidd refers in the novel itself,[13] has experienced tremendous loss for as long as she can remember, leaving her with such a grievous heart wound that it is a wonder she is not yet jaded or closed off. Instead, she is split open . . . wide open throughout her travail. Lily does not leave even the first paragraph without noticing how the way the bees that squeezed through the cracks of her bedroom wall "flew, not even looking for a flower, [just bee-ing] just flying for the feel of the wind," and it just "split [her heart] down its seam."[14] Such freedom in being, of course, would touch Lily's sorrowful soul. She longs for peace, understanding, even that peace which passes the need for understanding, that intrinsic mystery of being able to *live* in peace, finding shelter for her spirit and comfort for her soul.

Motherlessness is Lily's loss, but it is more than even that. Lily endures a double grief, a kind of hyper queenlessness, just stripped of sustenance, no mother, yes, but also and ironically the guilt and horror that she herself, even if accidentally, killed her own mother.

She carries not only the devastation that her mother abandoned her, proving her unlovable, she believes, but when her mother did return to try to reclaim her and to face the brutal abuser, who was her father, Lily in an attempt to rescue her mother accidentally shot her. Lily carries a multiple and layered mother wound, that of abandonment by her mother and guilt for murdering or abandoning, as she believes, the abandoner. A mental and emotional double bind extraordinaire. These losses must be grieved for any kind of restoration or rebirth of Lily's life to take hold. They are the driving force that informs the novel and Lily's deep desire to find a way to live her life in spite of such damage. They pervade her imagination, her psyche, and the entire text, this mother wound. It is this vulnerability, though, through which she finds compassion for others and a lens through which her insight and imagination are empowered. This is not surprising from Kidd, who declared in her "Life Is A Story" lecture that a classic feminine journey would be nothing less.[15]

In "Why It's Crucial for Women to Heal the Mother Wound," from her e-book *Womb of Light: The Power of the Awakened Feminine*, Bethany Webster asserts that

> for every human being, the very first wound of the heart was at the site of the mother, the feminine. And through the process of healing that wound, our hearts graduate from a compromised state of defensiveness and fear to a whole new level of love and power, which connects us to the divine heart of Life itself. We are from then on connected to the archetypal, collective heart that lives in all beings, and are carriers and transmitters of true compassion and love that the world needs. . . . In this way the mother wound is actually an opportunity and an invitation into the divine feminine.[16]

Is this not like St. Augustine in *The City of God,* noted by Mathewes in his lecture on "Public Religion in Imperial Rome (Books 6 – 7)," recognizing that all that is is always inside God, that God is with us, not separate and apart from us?[17] Is this not also the Divine

Immanence for which Kidd reaches in her attempt, as Emanuel notes, "to find a feminine face of God,"[18] since for Kidd "Divine Immanence . . . represents the matriarchal view of spirituality,"[19] asserting, as she does, in *Dance of the Dissident Daughter,* that "Divine Immanence" is here, near, and now, "inherent in the material stuff of life" and not apart from it?[20] Is this not the empathy in Kidd's work, informed, she admits, by Emerson's concept of the common heart that humanity shares?[21] Is this not also the kind of awareness or expanded consciousness that would give rest and solace to any weary, heavy-laden traveler ready to lay down his or her burdens and walk the way with more lightness of being in the present moment?

Clearly, this divine feminine is exactly the mystical presence August celebrates in the ritual she has devised that centers on the Queen of Beings, the Queen Bee, as it were, Mary, the mother of Jesus. Her Eucharistic ceremony is patterned after a Catholic communion service. As August tells Lily, "[we] take our mother's Catholicism and mix in our own ingredients,"[22] inviting worship and devotion to the mother who gave birth to love itself and is the source of life, the feminine, elevating Mary to more than "just a vessel for the Christ child."[23] A unification of two different theologies, it appears, revealed when Lily asks August if she is Catholic, and her answer is both yes and no, another clear incongruent combination, another perception that is widened to integrate seeming polarities without apology, another bit of the inscrutable in this secret life.

Mary Day, as it was called, was a Feast Day, but somewhat unlike the Feast Days in a Christian tradition, it does not begin until all are fed first. More like dessert, Rosaleen brought out the "manna," if you will, "the platter of honey cakes,"[24] and August, fulfilling the role of the high priestess, motions for them to stand in a circle. Hebb even names the central religious image in *Bees* as the honey, a metaphor for healing,[25] and August had told Lily that when bees were around, it meant a person's soul would be reborn in the next life.[26] Moreover, Hebb goes on to say that some medieval hymns referenced the Virgin Mary as "the beehive, and Christ as the honey that flowed from her."[27] "These are Mary's honey cakes," August begins, "Honey cakes for the Queen of Heaven."[28] Then, similar to an Anglican or Catholic litany, she pinches off a piece of the honey cake and turns to the first person in the circle and chants in true ecclesiastical mode, "This is the body of the Blessed Mother,"[29] and, as Lily says, "popped it in" the person's mouth. Then that person in turn turns to the person next to him or her and does the same until "the circle of feeding"[30] is complete. Next, our Lady of Chains, the lore about which August had already introduced to Lily in the early weeks, when she had first come to the pink house, is carried forth for all to hear the retelling of her story, a story within the larger story, possibly implying a theological notion that within all theologies is this divine feminine, the very source or wellspring or womb room of life, the great unifier of all things and lover of all things, the bearer of all things, this mother of all mysteries, at the heart of the matter.

No wonder the Bible-based Sunday services had all been devoted to Mary, this Black Madonna, and were led again by the august pastoral figure, August herself, reciting, "And Mary said . . . Behold, from henceforth all generations shall call me Blessed. For he that is mighty has done to me great things. . . ."[31] These "great things" in August's common prayer are quite specific, however, in their allusion to how the slaves on the islands near Charleston had prayed to the Lord for rescue, consolation, and freedom, and one day Obadiah had found the wooden figure washed up on the bank with "arm lifted out and fist balled up."[32] "Obadiah knew the Lord had sent this figure,"[33] but it is Pearl, the oldest of the slaves, who declares, "This here is the mother of Jesus."[34] Moreover, "this here" places the novel in "the long western tradition of mystical discourse, the pursuit in words of what is beyond words."[35] The story is specific to these individuals, but it is about revering that power which is much greater than they are as individual selves, the collective heart of all beings, the divine heart of Life itself, and yet to reach it, the kind of language they would understand is needed, even though it is a narrative about that which passes understanding. Again, in Abbott's view, "A real mystery [is] where the inexplicable meets the need to relieve it."[36]

Again, in the light of St. Augustine's assertion in the *City of God* that humans need to worship,[37] as Mathewes relates in "Splendid Vices and Happiness in Hope (Book 5)," the same seems particularly obvious in a world where society isolates, alienates, and segregates people, as these women bask in this resonating rite that one of their own created to fulfill that need to adore the ineffable, embodied in a feminine figure to whom they can specifically relate and from whom they can simultaneously evoke what Abbott would call "divine illumination."[38] This seems to be a recognition from Kidd that while this need humans have to humble themselves before that which is holy and stand in awe of the love that bears all things for all people, the great unfathomable is at the end of the day best expressed in the eternal maternal.

The narrative of this mother, this Mary, this Lady of Chains, develops: "Everyone knew the mother of Jesus was named Mary, and that she'd seen suffering of every kind. That she was strong and constant and had a mother's heart."[39] Not only that, but she had been chained by the master in the barn fifty times, but fifty times she had escaped and gone home. She not only had broken free, but she found her way to the place of soul comfort. They called her Our Lady of Chains not because she wore chains but because she broke free of them.[40] She found a way to live unbridled, a way to authentically be. This is the human hope. And it is surely Lily's.

So goes the liturgical script to which August adheres in the service, serving up hope for reaching the "cognitive sublime."[41] Each "time the master chained Mary in the carriage house, she would break the chains and return to her people."[42] August would then lift her voice to sanctify: "What is bound will be unbound. What is cast down will be lifted up."[43] Yes, this is about freedom, but it is also about rebirth, even a resurrection or regeneration to a way of being in the midst of a world of suffering, not giving that suffering the final or only say but confirming that while one can be taken down repeatedly by others as well as self, still one can rise, still one can be devoted to love. After the service, Lily muses, "You could die in a river, but maybe you could get reborn in it, too, like the bee-hive tombs August told me about."[44] Lily could now come to terms with her mother's abandonment and her own abandonment and the truth of having killed her own mother—and still find peace. Trappist monk Thomas Merton, Catholic writer, theologian, and mystic to whom Kidd refers as having changed her own thinking,[45] says, "The basic and most fundamental problem of the spiritual life is the acceptance of our hidden and dark self."[46] Is this not what Lily does? Merton goes on to name "the sacred attitude then [as] one of deep and fundamental respect for the real in whatever new form it may present itself."[47] A way of having that fundamental respect for the real can now be available to Lily.

Could this attitude be the source of that transcendent joy which Augustine submits that human beings long for, as noted by Mathewes in his lecture "The Price of Empire (Books 2-3)" on *The City of God*?[48] Is this first of all the admittance, without judg-ment or condemnation, of the sinner, who lies within all, to which Augustine refers?[49] Is it possible August's name is actually an allu-sion to Augustine? Is this a Christian-based Goddess as godhead? Is this a kind of world-making to which Abbott refers when narrative moves require a "cognitive recalibration?"[50] The theme threads its way throughout the novel, in a way similar to how Gabriel Garcia Marquez reveals that legend and myth-making and even history are created. These women create something in which they can believe, an idealized figure that meets their need to put their faith in some-thing far greater than themselves. Can this way lead to the secret of being in union with the immutable, not looking for anything in particular and instead just living for the sheer experience of it? Like the bees?

But first comes truth, which Lily musters the courage to con-front when she takes the first step to escape her father's household, breaks Rosaleen out of jail at all costs, and flees to Tiburon to ul-timately confront her own dialectical reality: "I loved myself, and

I hated myself. That's what the Black Madonna did to me, made me feel my glory and my shame at the same time."[51] She can hardly bear to see the shackled Mary, but August is there to mother her. "It is only a re-enactment . . . to help us remember."[52] Following that August iterates one of the central ideas in the novel: "Remembering is everything."[53] The power is within, but it requires the courage to face the past head-on. At that moment it becomes apparent that memory holds the seeds of an awakening consciousness and a healed heart. Therein lies the guidance and the hope for Lily: that in facing the whole truth, rather than a one-sided version of it, awareness and understanding and the heart and soul can all be expanded. Then a new way of being that can love self and others, embrace contradictions in all things without condemnation, and fully accept life, is possible.

It is August who shows her the threshold: "Our Lady is not some magical being out there somewhere, like a fairy godmother. She's *not* the statue in the parlor. She's something *inside* of you. . . . You have to find a mother inside yourself. We all do. Even if we already have a mother, we still have to find this part of ourselves inside."[54] In *your own heart.*[55] Therein lies the home you seek. "She's the power inside you, you understand?"[56] "And when you get down to it, Lily, that's the only purpose grand enough for a human life. Not just to love—but to *persist* in love."[57] Before that in the honey house, this beekeeper, who knows the ways of being in this world, mothers Lily the way she had mothered Lily's mother before her. This wise and grand spiritual mother August gives Lily the bigger unifying truth in love; "We're all so human," she says. "Your mother made a terrible mistake, but she tried to fix it. . . . There is nothing perfect. . . . There is only life."[58]

August has pursued this moment of revelation with patience, making space for Lily to trust her, as they forged the bond of belonging to one another over time, mentoring Lily in life lessons learned amid her epistemological keeping of the bees. She keeps "bee-ing" at the forefront of her concerns, bringing Lily to the place in her own heart where she can face and accept the contradictions in herself, as she takes responsibility for her own inevitable human shortcomings, knowing all is never completely known in a world of ambiguity. Only one thing is certain: she cannot resist love, having first blurted out to August that she loved her[59] and subsequently accepting August's truth that then she, Lily herself, is indeed enough.[60] Certainly, this is when Lily finds what Emanuel calls her "spiritual center."[61]

Those are the paces that Lily must take, so that she can, like the early followers of Mary, who believed in "self-empowerment and sought the God within each of them," find the mother, the peace, the freedom, "the God-force"[62] inside to be herself and fly like the bees—but not before her final redemptive confession: "I have forgiven us both, although sometimes in the night my dreams will take me back to sadness, and I have to wake up and forgive us again."[63] Now, the power to remember her life in light of August's eschatology that "Life gives way to death and then death turns around and gives way to life"[64] gives Lily the guidance to walk in love and the way of perpetual renewal, like the bees, re-queening herself to be free and light and purposeful in the ultimate reality of wholeness and holiness of just being . . . herself.

Richard Tarnas, in *The Passion of the Western Mind*, believes "*the deepest passion of the Western mind has been to reunite with the ground of its own being.*"[65] Is this not a ruling inclination in *The Secret Life of Bees*, if not the secret itself? However, Tarnas further asserts that

> the driving impulse of the West's masculine consciousness has been its dialectical quest not only to realize itself, to forge its own autonomy, but also, finally, to come to terms with the great feminine principle in life, and thus to recover its connection with the whole: to differentiate itself from but then rediscover and reunite with the feminine, with the mystery of life, of nature, of soul.[66]

Surely Sue Monk Kidd and her *Secret Life of Bees* belongs and contributes to furthering such discourse. In fact, Tarnas goes on to further reiterate how

[t]hat reunion can now occur on a new and profoundly different level from that of the primordial unconscious unity, for [what he called] the long evolution of human consciousness has prepared it to be capable at last of embracing its own ground and matrix freely and consciously. The *telos*, the inner direction and goal of the Western mind, has been to reconnect with the cosmos in a mature *participation mystique*, to surrender itself freely and consciously in this embrace of a larger unity that preserves human autonomy while also transcending human alienation.[67]

Is this not the paradoxical unity, pragmatic phenomenology, and ontological equanimity required to make life simply divine in *The Secret Life of Bees*?

NOTES

1. Sue Monk Kidd, *The Secret Life of Bees* (New York: Penguin, 2002), 222.
2. Catherine Emanuel, "The Archetypal Mother: The Black Madonna in Sue Monk Kidd's *The Secret Life of Bees*," *West Virginia Philological Papers*, 52 (2005): 116, Literature Resource Center, http://go.galegroup.com.yosemite.wbu.edu/ps/i.do?ty=as&v=2.1&u=txshracd2627&it=DIourl&s=RELE-VANCE&p=LitRC&qt=TI-%22The%20archetypal%20mother%3A%20the%20Black%20Madonna%20in%20Sue%20Monk%20Kidd%27s%20The%20Secret%20Life%20of%20Bees%22--AU-Emanuel%2C%20Catherine%20B.--PU-%22West%20Virginia%20University%20Philological%20Papers%22--VO-52&lm=&sw=w.
3. Kidd, *The Secret Life of Bees*, 289.
4. Sue Monk Kidd, "Life Is a Story," YouTube video, 00:60, from Westminster Forum February 11, 2014, posted by MySPNN, February 25, 2014, https://www.youtube.com/watch?v=152Prmb1IK8.
5. Charles Mathewes, "Sacrifice and Ritual (Book 10)," *Books That Matter: The City of God*, The Great Courses Plus on Roku. 30 minutes, March 2017.
6. Kidd, *The Secret Life of Bees*, 147.
7. Kidd, *The Secret Life of Bees*, 147.
8. H. Porter Abbott, *Real Mysteries, Narrative and the Unknowable* (Columbus: The Ohio State University Press, 2013),11.

9. Judith Hebb, "Religious Imagery in *The Secret Life of Bees* and *The Mermaid Chair, Contemporary Literary Criticism* 267 (2009): 1, Literature Resource Center, go.galegroup.com/ps/i.do?p=LitRC&sw=w&u=txshracd 2627&v=2.1&id=GALE%7CH1100089620&it=r&asid=e4f51c66fc0cb-6ce7304b279b71d8754.

10. Emanuel, "The Archetypal Mother: The Black Madonna in Sue Monk Kidd's *The Secret Life of Bees*," 115.

11. Cindy Crossby, "PW Talks with Sue Monk Kidd Remembering the Spirit," *Publishers Weekly* 253.27 (2006): 73, Literature Resource Center, http://eds.a.ebscohost.com.yosemite.wbu.edu/eds/results?vid=0&sid=782 741a978dc4600b1f139b7162632f1%40session-mgr4008&bquery=TI+((Sue+AND+Monk+AND+Kidd+AND+Remembering+AND+the+AND+Spirit))&bdata=JmNsaTA9RlQmY2x2MD1ZJ-nR5cGU9MCZzaXRlPWVkcy1saXZl.

12. Charles Mathewes, "Splendid Vices and Happiness in Hope (Book 5)," *Books That Matter:* The City of God, The Great Courses Plus on Roku, 30 minutes, March 2017.

13. Kidd, *The Secret Life of Bees*, 130.

14. Kidd, *The Secret Life of Bees*, 1.

15. Kidd, "Life Is a Story."

16. Bethany Webster, *Womb of Light: The Power of the Awakened Feminine*, WordPress.com, EBook, (http://www.womboflight.com).

17. Charles Mathewes, "Public Religion in Imperial Rome (Books 6-7)," *Books That Matter: The City of God*, The Great Courses Plus on Roku, 30 minutes, March 2017.

18. Emanuel, "The Archetypal Mother," 115.

19. Emanuel, "The Archetypal Mother," 116.

20. Sue Monk Kidd, *The Dance of the Dissident Daughter* (San Francisco: Harper Collins, 2002), 160.

21. Kidd, "Life Is a Story."

22. Kidd, *The Secret Life of Bees*, 90.

23. Emanuel, "The Archetypal Mother," 118.

24. Kidd, *The Secret Life of Bees*, 225.

25. Hebb, "Religious Imagery in *The Secret Life of Bees* and *The Mermaid Chair*," 7.

26. Kidd, *The Secret Life of Bees*, 206.

27. Hebb, "Religious Imagery in *The Secret Life of Bees* and *The Mermaid Chair*," 7.

28. Kidd, *The Secret Life of Bees*, 226.

29. Kidd, *The Secret Life of Bees*, 226.

30. Kidd, *The Secret Life of Bees*, 226.
31. Kidd, *The Secret Life of Bees*, 107.
32. Kidd, *The Secret Life of Bees*, 108.
33. Kidd, *The Secret Life of Bees*, 108.
34. Kidd, *The Secret Life of Bees*, 109.
35. Abbott, *Real Mysteries,* 28.
36. Abbott, *Real Mysteries,* 3.
37. Charles Mathewes, "Splendid Vices and Happiness in Hope (Book 5)," *Books That Matter: The City of God,* The Great Courses Plus on Roku, 30 minutes, March 2017.
38. Abbott, *Real Mysteries,* 32.
39. Kidd, *The Secret Life of Bees*, 109.
40. Kidd, *The Secret Life of Bees*, 110.
41. Abbott, *Real Mysteries,* 53.
42. Kidd, *The Secret Life of Bees*, 228.
43. Kidd, *The Secret Life of Bees*, 228.
44. Kidd, *The Secret Life of Bees*, 229.
45. Kidd, "Life Is a Story."
46. Thomas Merton, *The Pocket Thomas Merton* (Boston: New Seeds, 2005), 155.
47. Merton, *The Pocket Thomas Merton,* 156.
48. Charles Mathewes, "The Price of Empire (Books 2-3)," *Books That Matter: The City of God,* The Great Courses Plus on Roku, 30 minutes, March 2017.
49. Charles Mathewes, "Your Passport to *The City of God*," *Books That Matter: The City of God,* The Great Courses Plus on Roku, 30 minutes, March 2017.
50. Abbott, *Real Mysteries,* 74.
51. Kidd, *The Secret Life of Bees*, 71.
52. Kidd, *The Secret Life of Bees*, 228.
53. Kidd, *The Secret Life of Bees*, 228.
54. Kidd, *The Secret Life of Bees*, 288.
55. Kidd, *The Secret Life of Bees*, 288.
56. Kidd, *The Secret Life of Bees*, 289.
57. Kidd, *The Secret Life of Bees*, 289.
58. Kidd, *The Secret Life of Bees*, 256.
59. Kidd, *The Secret Life of Bees*, 284.
60. Kidd, *The Secret Life of Bees*, 289.
61. Emanuel, "The Archetypal Mother," 118.
62. Emanuel, "The Archetypal Mother," 118.

63. Kidd, *The Secret Life of Bees*, 301.

64. Kidd, *The Secret Life of Bees*, 206.

65. Richard Tarnas, *The Passion of the Western Mind, Understanding the Ideas That Have Shaped Our World View* (New York: Random House, 1991), 443.

66. Tarnas, *The Passion of the Western Mind*, 443.

67. Tarnas, *The Passion of the Western Mind*, 443-444.

BIBLIOGRAPHY

Abbott, H. Porter. *Real Mysteries: Narrative and the Unknowable.* Columbus: The Ohio State University Press, 2013.

Crossby, Cindy. "PW Talks with Sue Monk Kidd Remembering the Spirit."*Publishers Weekly* 253.27 (2006): 73. Literature Resource Center. http://eds.a.ebscohost.com.yosemite.wbu.edu/eds/re-sults?vid=0&sid=782741a978dc4600b1f139b7162632f1%40sessionmgr4 008&bquery=TI+((Sue+AND+Monk+AND+Kidd+AND+Remembering +AND+the+AND+Spirit))&bdata=JmNsaTA9RlQmY2x2MD1ZJnR5c-GU9MCZzaXRlPWVkcy1saXZl.

Emanuel, Catherine. "The Archetypal Mother: The Black Madonna in Sue Monk Kidd's *The Secret Life of Bees*." *West Virginia Philological Papers* 52 (2005): 115-122. Literature Resource Center. http://go.galegroup.com. yosemite.wbu.edu/ps/i.do?ty=as&v=2.1&u=txshracd2627&it=DIourl& s=RELEVANCE&p=LitRC&qt=TI-%22The%20archetypal%20mother% 3A%20the%20Black%20Madonna%20in%20Sue%20Monk%20Kidd% 27s%20The%20Secret%20Life%20of%20Bees%22~~AU~Emanuel% 2C%20Catherine%20B.~~PU~%22West%20Virginia%20University%20 Philological%20Papers%22~~VO~52&lm=&sw=w.

Hebb, Judith. "Religious Imagery in *The Secret Life of Bees* and *The Mermaid Chair*." *Contemporary Literary Criticism* 267 (2009). Literature Resource Center. go.galegroup.com/ps/i.do?p=LitRC&sw=w&u=tshracd2627& v=2.1&id=GALE%7CH1100089620&it=r&asid=e4f51c66fc0cb-6ce7304b279b71d8754.

Kidd, Sue Monk. "Life Is a Story." YouTube video, 00:60, from Westminster Forum February 11, 2014, posted by MySPNN, February 25, 2014. https://www.youtube.com/watch?v=152Prmb1IK8.

———. *The Dance of the Dissident Daughter.* San Francisco: Harper Collins, 2002.

———. *The Secret Life of Bees.* New York: Penguin, 2002.

Mathewes, Charles. "Public Religion in Imperial Rome (Books 6-7)." *Books That Matter: The City of God.* The Great Courses Plus on Roku, 30 minutes. March 2017.

———. "Sacrifice and Ritual (Book 10)." *Books That Matter: The City of God.* The Great Courses Plus on Roku, 30 minutes. March 2017.

———. "Splendid Vices and Happiness in Hope (Book 5)." *Books That Matter: The City of God.* The Great Courses Plus on Roku, 30 minutes. March 2017.

———. "The Price of Empire (Books 2-3)." *Books That Matter: The City of God.* The Great Courses Plus on Roku, 30 minutes. March 2017.

———. "Your Passport to *The City of God.*" *Books That Matter: The City of God.* The Great Courses Plus on Roku, 30 minutes. March 2017.

Merton, Thomas. *The Pocket Thomas Merton.* Boston: New Seeds, 2005.

Tarnas, Richard. *The Passion of the Western Mind, Understanding the Ideas That Have Shaped Our World View.* New York: Random House, 1991.

Webster, Bethany. *Womb of Light: The Power of the Awakened Feminine.* WordPress.com. EBook. http://www.womboflight.com.

FIVE

The Power of Poetic Perception in *The Secret Life of Bees*

DEBORAH J. KUHLMANN

I n *The Poetics of Space* Gaston Bachelard submits the notion that "Contemporary poetry . . . has introduced freedom in the very body of the language. As a result, poetry appears as a phenomenon of freedom."[1] Furthermore, images themselves hold a "poetic significance," for "poetry is there with its countless surging images, images through which the creative imagination comes to live in its own domain."[2] In *The Secret Life of Bees* by Sue Monk Kidd poetic images abound in the "shimmering consciousness"[3] of the protagonist, Lily Owens, from whose point of view secrets are revealed. Lily, the white, motherless, adolescent daughter left with an abusive father, seeks not only freedom from brutality but a home for her heart. She longs for the love of a mother who abandoned her as well as relief from the terrible burden of guilt she carries for having accidentally shot and killed that very mother, Deborah, when she returned and Lily tried but failed to rescue her. It is a twisted and harsh irony Lily endures. It is a wonder she can, but she does. She not only finds the courage to escape but to bust the closest person she has to a parent, Rosaleen, out of jail. A black woman and "stand-in mother,"[4] as Lily calls her, Rosaleen was jailed for standing up to a white man and then defiantly pouring her jug of spit right on his shoe in the heat of the civil-rights-era South. Lily manages to get them both to another town, where they find shelter with a black family: property-owning August and her sisters May and June Boatwright. August in particular becomes Lily's mentor-mother, spiritual guide, and high priestess to healing and wholeness. It is an arduous journey, requiring courage, forgiveness, truth-telling, forging commitments, and relentlessly persisting in love.[5] At every step that will take Lily to another chance to grow, risk is involved, and fear must be confronted. She makes her way to peace and tranquility, not perfection. At times the challenges can be overwhelming, but it is her poetic perception that sees her through, gives her respite in times of trouble, and ultimately gives the freedom of being she so desires.

In fact, it is in those moments or poetic instants when she finds release, not so much *from* the difficulty she is facing but by engaging *in* primal actuality. Bachelard notes that "the imagination [is] a major power of human nature."[6] Furthermore, "the values that belong to daydreaming mark humanity in its depths. Daydreaming even has a privilege of autovalorization. It derives pleasure from its own being."[7] Lily is a daydreamer, and we, the reader, get to see the world and experience it through the lens of her poetic imagination. A psychologist might argue this is her escape from reality. But Bachelard contends that "the poetic image places us at the origin of the speaking being,"[8] for the poetic imagination "involves bringing about a veritable awakening of poetic creation, even in the soul . . . through the reverberations of a single poetic image."[9] Moreover, it is "through this reverberation, by going immediately beyond all psychology or psychoanalysis, [that] we feel a poetic power rising . . . within us."[10] He even goes so far as to say "poetry possesses a felicity of its own, however great the tragedy it may be called upon to illustrate."[11] In short, poetry is transcendent, regardless. Bachelard calls it "exalting reality."[12] And ultimately he says "the essential newness of the poetic image poses the problem of the speaking being's creativeness. Through this creativeness the imagining consciousness proves to be, very simply but very purely, an origin."[13] "[F]or a simple poetic image . . . a flicker of the soul is all that is needed."[14] A supreme power, he says, is here; "it is human dignity."[15] And, therefore, where the poet speaks is "on the threshold of being."[16] Kidd herself confirms her own spirituality "as an unfolding process . . . that is about an expansion of the heart and soul and mind, and coming into deeper relationship not only with the divine but with one's self"[17] in an interview in 2006. She relates how she took an understanding of what she calls "deep being"— being at the core of oneself and how to dwell there—from Buddhism.[18] It is this being that is mirrored in *The Secret Life of Bees*.

It is on the threshold to this inner space of essential being where Lily engages her daydream reveries infused with poetic images that emerge as direct products of her heart, soul, and presence, "apprehended in . . . actuality."[19] In this sense Lily is not escapist but is engaging in life and existence itself, where this epiphanic power renders a "transformation of being" in a heartbeat.[20]

Even in the opening paragraph Lily tells us her version of the bee show she watched while lying in bed:

> how bees squeezed through the cracks . . and flew circles
> around the room . . . their wings shining like bits of chrome . . .
> The way those bees flew, not even looking for a flower, just
> flying for the feel of the wind, split my heart down its seam.[21]

This is Lily's point of view, but the novel could arguably be told from the perspective of the poetic imagination itself in those images that bring Lily right to the edge of an awakened consciousness, the way to overcome, if you will, the personal and slide right into that which is greater than self. At one point Lily "for a moment" relates how she "lost [her] boundaries, feeling like the sky was [her] own skin and the moon was [her] heart beating up there in the dark . . . the air making moisture on [her] chest and the sky puckering with light."[22] And later, fleeing T. Ray's (her father's) house, she says, "I disappeared into violet light cobwebbed air."[23] According to Richard Kearney in the "Introduction" of *The Poetics of Space*,

"The highest act of imagination is the will . . . [not to run from but] . . . to attune oneself to the saying of being itself."[24] Surely this is Lily continuously celebrating what Kearney refers to as "Not non-being but surplus-being; being as incessant birthing of newness through images."[25]

There are countless examples. Day one of her new life is just one: "I woke beside the creek in a bed of kudzu vines. A barge of mist floated along the water, and dragonflies, iridescent blue ones, darted back and forth like they were stitching up the air."[26] Her poetic imagination continues to evoke her increased awareness, immersing herself in being present to each moment of experience:

> We drifted by gray barns, cornfields in need of irrigation, and clumps of Hereford cows, chewing in slow motion, looking very content with their lives . . . into the distance . . . farmhouses with wide porches and tractor-tire swings suspended from ropes on nearby tree branches; windmills sprouted up beside them, their giant silver petals creaking a little when the breezes rose. The sun . . . baked everything to perfection; even the goose berries on the fence had fried to raisins.[27]

Similar to a Wordsworthian intent and aligned with Bachelard, this poet's impressions deliver the extraordinary in the ordinary, "stirring being into language and language into being," as she finds "the mystical in matter."[28]

Even Lily herself, when seeing August for the first time, describes the experience as "awe for the mystery playing out."[29] This emergence of such an august luminary into Lily's life is reflected in the visual rendering, the one she both receives and creates at once. Her attention is locked and centered on her subject, and therefore is able at the same time to participate in remaking the material image. As Kearney observes,

> Poetics is about hearing and feeling as well as crafting and shaping. It is the double play of re-creation. And this oscillating tension flies in the face of traditional dichotomies between subject

and object, mind and matter, active and passive, which inform the history of Western thought. Or to put it another way: Bachelard's sense of poetic creation transcends the traditionally opposed roles of image as either "imitation" or "invention."[30]

For Bachelard, imagination is at once both receptive and creative. The two functions are inseparable.[31] Lily's vision of August illustrates this confluence in poetry as well as her own lyrical and imaginative mindset, which delivers her in that instant from the bondage of her personal miseries:

> The woman moved along a row of white boxes that bordered the woods beside the pink house, a house so pink it remained a scorched shock on the back of my eyelids after I looked away. She was tall, dressed in white, wearing a pith helmet with veils that floated across her face, settled around her shoulders, and trailed down her back. She looked like an African bride. Lifting the tops off the boxes, she peered inside, swinging a tin bucket of smoke back and forth. Clouds of bees rose up and flew wreaths around her head. Twice she disappeared in the fogged billows, then gradually reemerged like a dream rising up from the bottom of the night.[32]

Intertwining spirits, one observed, the other observing, become one as the manifestation of being is captured in the artistic depiction, "a pure product of absolute imagination," which Bachelard asserts is itself "a phenomenon of being."[33] Such "imaginative contact with the outer world renews our inner being,"[34] according to Kearney, and breaks like every other true poetic image, according to Bachelard, with linear clock time, surprising "at the moment of emergence" into the waking consciousness.[35] Such is Lily's moment of awe at seeing August.

Many more examples abound throughout the novel. Here are just a few:

- Zach driving the honey wagon, as "the wind whipped my hair and flooded the truck with a weedy, new-mown smell."[36]

- The roadsides "covered with fresh-picked cotton, blown from the trucks carrying it to the gin in Tiburon."[37]
- The cotton "scattered along the highway, it looked for all the world like snow . . . made me wish for a blizzard to come cool things down."[38]
- "I went off into a daydream" . . . "I imagined . . . building a snow cave, sleeping with our bodies twined together to get warm, our arms and legs like black-and-white braids."[39]

Clearly, these snapshots in Lily's mindset and outlook are like the poetics to which Bachelard adheres, as they are "not a matter of anonymous floating signifiers"; instead they "signal relational dynamics between beings, involving vital dimensions of intimacy, secrecy, desire, and repose."[40] They are always about connection and communion, not division and disunity.

The Secret Life of Bees is told from the point of view of a poet. All the reflections and daydreams are her connection to and expression of the eternal now, not an escape from it. And that is the secret, as it surely appears to be, of *The Secret Life of Bees*.

Again, Kearney adds relevant support:

> Imagination is at its best when it is incarnate, elemental, opening out into time and space, even when the space is elsewhere—before being, beneath being, more than being. For Bachelard, images are not merely seen but lived. They are not just vision, but the cosmos itself as it expands and amplifies from the minute to the magnified, creating concordance of world immensity with intimate depth of being.[41]

Consider a cluster of beehives. Lily says,

> According to August, if you've never seen a cluster of [them] first thing in the morning, you missed the eighth wonder of the world. Picture these white boxes tucked under pine trees. The sun will slant through the branches, shining in the sprinkles of dew drying on the lids . . . a few hundred bees doing laps

around the hive boxes, just warming up . . . From a distance
like a big painting . . . in a museum . . . Fifty feet away you will
hear it, a humming that sounds like it came from another planet.
At thirty feet your skin . . . [starts] . . . to vibrate. The hair . . .
[lifts] . . . on your neck. Your head will say, *Don't go any farther*,
but your heart will send you straight into the hum, where you
will be swallowed by it. You will stand there and think, *I am the
center of the universe, where everything is sung to life.*[42]

Lily finds the joy and the freedom that was right there within herself all along.

Says Bachelard, "[A] sincere impulse toward admiration . . . is
always necessary if we are to receive the phenomenological benefit
of a poetic image."[43] "In this admiration, which goes beyond the
passivity of contemplative attitudes, the joy of reading appears to
be the reflection of the joy of writing . . . [and then] the reader participates in the joy of creation."[44] In any case, the harmony
achieved in poetic images is inseparable from admiration.[45] Understandable, for while the point of view in *The Secret Life of Bees*
stems from a poetically minded protagonist, her creator, Sue Monk
Kidd, though she presents her narrative in prose, is the actual poet.

Daniel Boscaljon, in "The 'Pierless' Faith of Emily Dickinson,"
observes that "whether interpreting opinions or reconstructing
possibilities, the first stanzas [of Dickinson's work] acclimate readers to descriptive language about a direct experience in which an
unverifiable truth emerges at the moment of its presentation."[46]
And Rosamund Stone Zander and Benjamin Zander in *The Art of
Possibility* describe moments when there is an "experience of integration" with the world that transcends the business of survival.[47]
Furthermore, "these are moments when we forget ourselves and
seem to become part of all being."[48] In literature it is in the poetic
where these moments are best delivered. Sue Monk Kidd finds poetic language to convey Lily's moments of integration, where her
mindset expands to be a part of all being. Transcendent and integral all at once, Lily stands as the possibility for how a human being

can rise up and overcome the stark, dark struggles he or she may face, not bound by circumstance. In large part this transcendence is within experience, fully present, rather than in resistance or denial. To surrender to the "what is" of reality in full acceptance of one's being in it is the way Lily walks, and that experience is rendered in the poetics of possibility.

Indeed, in "The Grammar of Salvation and the Poetics of Possibility in Donne's Holy Sonnets," Danielle A. St. Hilaire quotes Ramie Targoff from *John Donne, Body and Soul*, which could easily be applied to those purple passages from Lily in *The Secret Life of Bees*: "What gives his poetry and prose its tremendous vitality derives to no small degree from his desire to seize this moment and not the next, to isolate and then luxuriate in a particular instance in time, to be all there in body and soul."[49] St. Hilaire observes that "in stepping out of time into a poetic 'now,' [Donne] reconfigures the question of salvation around the idea of possibility in the present rather than certainty of a time to come, and by doing so he avoids risking the loss of that savable selfhood that would be the consequence either of damnation or of union with God."[50] St. Hilaire claims that for Donne, the space of "now" is the poetic present that actually "interrupts the flow of time."[51] And further, the "emphasis on the present moment as opposed to temporal progression in the Holy Sonnets thus enables him to change the terms of the problem he faces."[52] It is within the "now" of a poem's present tense that consciousness dwells in possibility.[53] Kidd's speaker is Lily, where only her poetic voice can release such moments. The present progressive tense of her verbs and even her declarative present tense "*I am the center of the universe, where everything is sung to life*"[54] delivers these moments. As St. Hilaire observes about Donne, his speaker

> seeks to step outside of the problem of temporality altogether. If the relation between God's eternal decree and the speaker's temporal experience confounds attempts to narrate it in language, Donne's speaker finds security in the imperative mood

and in poetic apostrophe, forms that create their own time, a temporality disconnected from the confusing intersection of divine and human time . . .⁵⁵

In these epiphanies Lily stands in her own time, rendering Kidd's poetic voice of pure being. For Kidd as well as for Lily, those moments are sacred.

Neal McGowan reminds us of the insight by Rowan Williams in *The Edge of Words*, "what the poet seeks to do is something quite close to provoking a crisis in the language she is using or the linguistic situation she is setting out, so that a new perception is pushed into being."⁵⁶ Lily in *The Secret Life of Bees* is always pushing and reaching for her life, for liberty and love, as she emerges from the terrors and trials she has experienced at home. Even when obstacles, challenges, threats, and doubts enter the picture for her, she finds periodically within herself the rich desire for wholeness and merger with the essence of life, if you will, and when she articulates those moments, it is only poetic language that will suffice. Perhaps Kidd, through Lily's shimmering consciousness in those passages, is expressing—i.e. pressing out or pushing—her new perception of being into being, and it is in art, the art of poetry and the poetic mindset, where such an ontological experience can be presented.

Neal McGowan in "As Much Light as It Will Take: On Poetic Language and Revelation" also argues "that poetic language provides a window into understanding how language can become revelation."⁵⁷ Furthermore, "through entering the linguistic world that poetry creates, we encounter presences that exceed simple definition. We see the 'radiance' that might have been obscured because of habituated blindness."⁵⁸ Indeed, it is the radiance of Being that inhabits, informs, and infiltrates the perspective of Sue Monk Kidd in *The Secret Life of Bees*. Even the title itself suggests a poetic play that the secret of Being can "be" known in "being" itself. Ultimately, then, Kidd suggests the know-ability of such a secret, but it exceeds language, and therefore paradoxically it is poetic language that delights in metaphor that is the most fitting method of presenting transcendent revelation.[59] McGowan declares that "poetic language reveals that our communication is really a 'catching up' (to use a phrase from Rowan Williams) with something that we cannot master or manage completely. Things, concepts, and especially persons are excess laden and irreducible. The language of poetry delights in the irreducibility of the world and its excesses."[60] The moments of Lily's "revelations" in *The Secret Life of Bees* are nothing short of an expansion of her consciousness as it encounters the irreducibility of the world. Always present then is the un-know-ability or "secret" of all things, for in Kidd's view unknowing is paradoxically that which can be known in the experience of mystery, where one encounters and embraces that which is greater than self—essentially, then, engaging the divine. In *The Secret Life of Bees,* Sue Monk Kidd calls all human beings to explore such rich and transcendent possibility.

NOTES

1. Gaston Bachelard, *The Poetics of Space*, trans. Maria Jolas (New York: Penguin, 2014), 12.
2. Bachelard, *The Poetics of Space*, 13.
3. Bachelard, *The Poetics of Space*, 12.
4. Sue Monk Kidd, *The Secret Life of Bees* (New York, Penguin, 2002), 2.
5. Kidd, *The Secret Life of Bees*, 289.
6. Bachelard, *The Poetics of Space*, 18.
7. Bachelard, *The Poetics of Space*, 28.
8. Bachelard, *The Poetics of Space*, 8.
9. Bachelard, *The Poetics of Space*, 7-8.
10. Bachelard, *The Poetics of Space*, 8.
11. Bachelard, *The Poetics of Space*, 14.
12. Bachelard, *The Poetics of Space*, 15.
13. Bachelard, *The Poetics of Space*, 9.
14. Bachelard, *The Poetics of Space*, 6.
15. Bachelard, *The Poetics of Space*, 7.
16. Bachelard, *The Poetics of Space*, 2.
17. Cindy Crossby, "PW Talks with Sue Monk Kidd Remembering the Spirit," *Publishers Weekly* 253, no. 27 (2006): 73, Literature Resource Center, http://eds.a.ebscohost.com.yosemite.wbu.edu/eds/results?vid=0&sid=782.

18. Crossby, "PW Talks with Sue Monk Kidd," 73.

19. Bachelard, *The Poetics of Space*, 3.

20. Richard Kearney, Introduction to *The Poetics of Space*, by Gaston Bachelard (New York: Penguin, 2014), Xix.

21. Kidd, *The Secret Life of Bees*, 1.

22. Kidd, *The Secret Life of Bees*, 42.

23. Kidd, *The Secret Life of Bees*, 42.

24. Kearney, Introduction to *The Poetics of Space*, xx.

25. Kearney, Introduction to *The Poetics of Space*, xx.

26. Kidd, *The Secret Life of Bees*, 57.

27. Kidd, *The Secret Life of Bees*, 59.

28. Kearney, Introduction to *The Poetics of Space*, xxii.

29. Kidd, *The Secret Life of Bees*, 67.

30. Kearney, Introduction to *The Poetics of Space*, xix – xx.

31. Kearney, Introduction to *The Poetics of Space*, xx.

32. Kidd, *The Secret Life of Bees*, 67.

33. Bachelard, *The Poetics of Space,* 96.

34. Kearney, Introduction to *The Poetics of Space*, xxv.

35. Kearney, Introduction to *The Poetics of Space*, xxii.

36. Kidd, *The Secret Life of Bees*, 124.

37. Kidd, *The Secret Life of Bees*, 124.

38. Kidd, *The Secret Life of Bees*, 124.

39. Kidd, *The Secret Life of Bees*, 124.

40. Kearney, Introduction to *The Poetics of Space*, xxv.

41. Kearney, Introduction to *The Poetics of Space*, xxv.

42. Kidd, *The Secret Life of Bees*, 286.

43. Bachelard, *The Poetics of Space,* 11.

44. Bachelard, *The Poetics of Space,* 11.

45. Bachelard, *The Poetics of Space,* 11.

46. Daniel Boscaljon, "The 'Pierless' Faith of Emily Dickinson," *Modern Believing* 59 (4): 312, *EBSCOhost*, search.ebscohost.com/login.aspx?direct=true&db=rfh&AN=ATLAn4396510&site=eds-live.

47. Rosamund Stone Zander and Benjamin Zander, *The Art of Possibility* (New York: Penguin, 2000), 20.

48. Zander and Zander, *The Art of Possibility*, 20.

49. Danielle St. Hilaire, "The Grammar of Salvation and the Poetics of Possibility in Donne's Holy Sonnets," *Studies in Philology* 114 (3): 591, *EBSCOhost*, doi:10.1353/sip.2017.0021.

50. St. Hilaire, "The Grammar of Salvation," 592.

51. St. Hilaire, "The Grammar of Salvation," 605.

52. St. Hilaire, "The Grammar of Salvation," 606.
53. St. Hilaire, "The Grammar of Salvation," 607.
54. Kidd, *The Secret Life of Bees*, 286.
55. St. Hilaire, "The Grammar of Salvation," 608.
56. Neal McGowan, "As Much Light as It Will Take: On Poetic Language and Revelation," *Anglican Theological Review* 100 (2): 314, *EBSCOhost*, search.ebscohost.com/login.aspx?direct=true&db=rh&AN=129525538&site=eds-live.
57. McGowan, "As Much Light as It Will Take," 314.
58. McGowan, "As Much Light as It Will Take," 319.
59. McGowan, "As Much Light as It Will Take," 321.
60. McGowan, "As Much Light as It Will Take," 317.

BIBLIOGRAPHY

Bachelard, Gaston. *The Poetics of Space*. Translated by Maria Jolas. New York: Penguin, 2014.

Boscaljon, Daniel. "The 'Pierless' Faith of Emily Dickinson." *Modern Believing* 59 (4): 303–317. *EBSCOhost*, search.ebscohost.com/login.aspx?direct=true&db=rfh&AN=ATLAn4396510&site=eds-live.

Crossby, Cindy. "PW Talks with Sue Monk Kidd Remembering the Spirit." *Publishers Weekly* 253, no. 27 (2006): 73. Literature Resource Center. http://eds.a.ebscohost.com.yosemite.wbu.edu/eds/results?vid=0&sid=782.

Kearney, Richard. Introduction to *The Poetics of Space,* by Gaston Bachelard, xvii – xxvii. New York: Penguin, 2014.

Kidd, Sue Monk. *The Secret Life of Bees*. New York: Penguin, 2002.

McGowan, Neal. "As Much Light as It Will Take: On Poetic Language and Revelation." *Anglican Theological Review* 100 (2): 311–326. *EBSCOhost*,search.ebscohost.com/login.aspx?direct=true&db=rl-h&AN=129525538&site=eds-live.

St. Hilaire, Danielle A. "The Grammar of Salvation and the Poetics of Possibility in Donne's Holy Sonnets." *Studies in Philology* 114 (3): 591–608. *EBSCOhost*, doi:10.1353/sip.2017.0021.

Zander, Rosamund Stone and Benjamin Zander. *The Art of Possibility*. New York: Penguin, 2000.

SIX

Humor and the Art of Survival in *The Secret Life of Bees*

ARCH MAYFIELD AND
DEBORAH J. KUHLMANN

"A well-developed sense of humor is the pole that adds balance to your steps as you walk the tightrope of life." —W. A. WARD

For Lily, Sue Monk Kidd's protagonist in *The Secret Life of Bees*, humor not only becomes an inroad to sanity and preservation of her own integrity when everything around her is coming apart, but her interior monologue also stands as the voice of the author's humor, giving Kidd a clear if not prominent position among contemporary southern women novelists who use humor. That said, southern literary humor, as identified by Jennifer Hughes in "The South, Humor and Race," "from the early frontier humorists such as Augustus Baldwin Longstreet and Henry Clay Lewis to large looming later figures like Mark Twain, Flannery O'Connor, and Zora Neale Hurston—tends to be vivacious, rough-and-tumble, and willing to engage with a regional history fraught with abjection, violence, and terror."[1] For sure the circumstances in which Lily finds herself are not absent of such hostility, which is the context that serves to heighten and fuel the hilarity of her gritty perspective. In "Women in the Postmodern South," J. A. Bryant declares moreover that "humor is the distinguishing mark of the contemporary southern woman's work."[2]

Kidd's character Lily, then, while standing on the tradition of previous writers, also catapults this author into the southern postmodern contemporary spotlight.

In the opening pages of Sue Monk Kidd's *The Secret Life of Bees*, fourteen-year-old Lily Owens introduces readers to T. Ray, the man whom the term *Daddy* just does not seem to fit. He is an emotionally cold, loud, angry, and abusive parent, but he is the only one she has. Lily's mother died when she was four years old, and in fact Lily lives with a fear that she herself had something to do with her mother's death. To say she is carrying a burden would be a monumental understatement. She does remember how her parents were fighting that day, and T. Ray had pulled out a gun. They wrestled and the gun fell to the floor. Four-year-old Lily picked it up and then heard a loud noise. T-Ray has never done anything to alleviate Lily's guilt, and even allowed her to take responsibility for her mother's death. Living with him has been no easy task and has demanded resourcefulness and determination and strength just to hold onto any kind of self-worth, but Lily does, and it is the humor in her self-talk, accessed by the reader from Lily's interior monologue, that accounts for much of her ability to gain a footing in the world. Bryant acknowledges "a revolutionary impulse among recent southern female writers" as well as "the South's society as a whole has been slow to acknowledge woman's right to speak as if she were fully human, to say nothing of her claim to full humanity itself."[3] Furthermore, that voice is often achieved by "using the device of first-person narrator to report honestly and out loud their story of suppressed ambition, fear, and humiliation—doing so, moreover, with a combination of vigor and humor that manages to be at once reassuring to the teller and openly defiant."[4] A vigorous and humorous truth spoken by Lily to herself or anyone else is no laughing matter. It is a serious tactic for Lily's survival, and a serious technique for Kidd as a postmodern southern feminist writer, who implements humor through her character Lily as a way to speak truth to power and oppression.

Lily explains how she manages to cope with T. Ray after a schoolteacher, Mrs. Henry, gave Lily some books to encourage her reading and writing: "Whenever I opened one, T. Ray said 'Who do you think you are, Julius Shakespeare?' The man sincerely thought that was Shakespeare's first name, and if you think I should have corrected him, you are ignorant about the art of survival."[5] This early scene clearly reveals a wise-beyond-her-years protagonist, well equipped to navigate her often inhospitable environment. As often as every two or three pages throughout the book, Lily humorously engages with her world, always surviving whatever the world brings her way. No doubt the engagement and the humor help define Lily's character, but the humor-producing engagement also places her in a larger pattern worthy of academic study.[6]

Eileen Gillooly in "Women and Humor" observes that "humorous writing by women has suffered greater critical neglect than other forms of literary production,"[7] which only serves to underscore the need to examine Lily's behavior, not from a Freudian clinical standpoint, but rather to survey Lily's humor as a coping skill—her own self-named "art of survival"[8]—as well as Sue Monk Kidd's art of giving voice to a tradition of female humor as "de-centering, dis-locating and de-stabilizing" cultural authority in order to survive, and so is "distinguished from traditional comic forms."[9] Kidd readily then claims a space in the art of female humor, which itself "much like minority humor . . . represents a tactic of personal survival, a political and psychological strategy for managing the anger and frustration arising from the experience of oppression."[10] In one swoop Lily both upholds the patriarchy's value of education and exposes the irony that this man who is allowed to keep her and her dreams down is himself ignorant. A "bit of a guerilla tactic" that stands on a principle of "radical disruption rather than regeneration"? Which undermines, even if only in her own mind, by a "sly, disguised mockery, an authority that cannot otherwise be successfully confronted"?[11] It would surely seem so.

Through Lily, Sue Monk Kidd provides a sharp example of how women writers have engaged women's humor to "transform the anger and frustration attendant upon . . . hardships into a source of humorous satisfaction, a composition of 'resentments,' affording to [the character and] the author both psychological relief and the aesthetic pleasure of its production."[12] Lily copes with T. Ray, as she finds relief even in her own mind by getting to tell herself the truth as narrator in this way. She nails him but within the confines, absurdities, and contradictions of the dominant "patriarchal values," weakening his authority by exposing it to ridicule. Rather than denouncing "the system" or T. Ray, who personifies the absurdity of a system that would support so malicious a parent, she just holds him and it up for judgment. In an opening volley, Lily describes T. Ray: "I had asked God repeatedly to do something about T Ray. He'd gone to church for forty years and was only getting worse. It seemed like this should tell God something."[13] She cuts right to the spiritual core, his soul, as it were.

Again, when T. Ray refuses to buy large brush hair rollers for Lily, she resorts to using juice cans to roll her hair before bedtime. She quips, " . . . all year I'd had to roll it [hair] on Welch's grape juice cans, which had nearly turned me into an insomniac . . . always having to choose between decent hair and a good night's sleep."[14] She does not negate the prevailing ideological conditions that would affirm the "primacy of female beauty,"[15] but deals both T. Ray and the system a double blow, as she buys into the need to attain that image but simultaneously undercuts him for not supporting her in achieving that, so that he becomes the one who is actually subverting the patriarchy, and she then achieves with a swift reversal the status of heroine, ridiculous and laughable as it is, going to any lengths, even using grape juice cans and going without sleep, all in the name of satisfying the image of beauty as defined by the world in which she finds herself. In short, through humor she "mimics [the] dominant cultural values in order to expose them as culturally constructed and laughable, thereby challenging their [and T. Ray's] authority."[16] Through humor Lily keeps her balance and her own worth intact. As narrator she finds her voice, making her a survivor even on the verge of being a thriver. Through her character Lily, Kidd demonstrates the extent to which humor is an art that can and has contributed to women being able to *say* what is true, exposing that which would prevent women from having such a voice as silly in itself.

Lily continues to defy both T. Ray and the social constructs in another reversal, or even chiasmus, which does not criticize or call into question the patriarchal notion of feminine modesty or the "inferiority of the female intellect" or the like, as she just asserts and articulates with gusto the distinct bodily realities of being female. Can we say she celebrates it? She certainly makes no bones about those "unmentionables," as she proceeds to mention them right out loud. It serves as a clever and laughable way to vaporize T. Ray, as he is quick to leave immediately. If Lily needs to escape from T. Ray, she just informs him, "'I thought I'd walk to town with Rosaleen tomorrow. I need to buy some sanitary supplies.' He accepted this without comment. T. Ray hated female puberty worse than anything."[17] Like a queen with a magic wand, with these few comments she makes him disappear, allowing her to escape. T. Ray flat flees the scene. Her tactic has worked, and the truth has set her free, at least for a little while. She outwits him. Her intelligence enables her to cope with her adversary by speaking what is real to the fantasy of a system or a person who would suggest or intimate she not do that. Moreover, she reveals Kidd's artful use of humor as part of the "hallmark of women's humorous production," which is "female subversion."[18]

Much later, after Lily and Rosaleen are on the lam and living with the beekeeping Boatwright sisters, Lily calls T. Ray to ask a very serious question: Does he know her well enough to at least know her favorite color? She calls collect. T. Ray accepts the call. The conversation alternates between T. Ray's raging profanity "'You're goddam right I'll accept it . . . Lily, where the hell are you? . . . I'm gonna tear your behind to pieces"[19] and Lily's calm and stoic comments: "Then without waiting for me to say P-turkey, he launched right in."[20] In this scene, part of the humor stems from effective distance, noted by John Morreall in *Taking*

Laughter Seriously: "[a value of humor lies in] giving us distance and perspective."[21] As heart-wrenching as the situation is with Lily trying to obtain—even extort—the answer, and with the enraged T. Ray spewing obscenity, the emotional distance between the two heightens the hilarity and also displays her strength in the face of such emotional violence—abuse that does not diminish her worth. Moreover, it is the role reversal that sets the frame for laughter, as T. Ray is exposed as a tantrum-throwing infant, unable to endure change, while Lily remains the steady adult or parent, unveiling then the ridiculousness of the situation.

It may be that T. Ray's dogged desire to hang onto an outdated reality and his abject inability to accept the fact that Lily has grown up and is no longer under his control stands as symbolic of a South unwilling to give up its "stronghold of patriarchy,"[22] even in the face of change, and so has become laughable, even a mockery. Bryant observes that "undoubtedly the South's society as a whole has been slow to acknowledge woman's right to speak as if she were fully human, to say nothing of her claim to full humanity itself," and cites Barbara Bennett's *Comic Visions, Female Voices: Contemporary Women Novelists and Southern Humor* as finding that it is that "major sin of omission" which "drives a revolutionary impulse among recent southern female writers."[23] While we cannot say for sure that Kidd intends Lily to be "a revolutionary," she certainly fills that bill. In any case such dark humor, which makes light of or brings to light the emotional violence and decay that has characterized the southern scene, is an "intrinsic part of southern writing,"[24] and so earns Kidd herself a spot among southern feminist humorists.

The extent to which Lily has survived her childhood with T. Ray comes late in the novel, when T. Ray appears in Tiburon ostensibly to take Lily back home to Sylvan. He displayed "the fat grin of a man who has been rabbit hunting all day long and has just now found his prey backed up in a hollow log with no way out."[25] Lily greets him with a pretense of cordiality, "Won't you come in?"[26] Her tone disarms him. A short while later, T. Ray is sitting in the Boatwrights' rocking chair, pulls out a knife, and begins to "carve up the arm of the rocking chair like he was all of eleven years old, putting his initials in a tree."[27] Again, it is a comic reversal of roles—Lily as welcoming, albeit reluctant, adult host and T. Ray as the initial-carving child. But it has a serious foundation, as she recognizes and chooses to treat his incivility with civility. Lily looks straight at the truth of things, and that is the basis of her humor. Her comedy is rooted in her bravery.

Lily copes with the rest of the world. Lily depends on humor as she confronts the sometimes uncomfortable, even painful, reality of the external world, exclusive of T. Ray. She remarks, for instance, on people's reaction when she refers to her mother's death: "My mother died when I was four years old. It was a fact of life but if I brought it up, people would suddenly get interested in their hangnails and cuticles, or else distant places in the sky."[28] Lily seems to recognize the irony of her being much more able to discuss her mother's death than are people around her, and comments on their inability with a comic twist. In this sense Kidd is in good company with renowned southern female writer Eudora Welty, whose own humor was a synthesis of both tragedy and comedy.[29] In "'We weren't laughing at them. . . .We're grieving with you': Empathy and Comic Vision in Welty's *The Optimist's Daughter*," Adrienne V. Akins identifies the connection between humor and empathy in Welty's brand of humor.[30] Similarly, a profound lack of empathy reveals the short supply of both compassion and comprehension among the adults in Lily's world. Trivial details of life, rather than empathy for Lily's grief, take center stage in her encounters with these adults, and the outcome is comic relief. The truth not only sets her free, but it also unleashes her humor. She holds back neither her humor nor her tears.

In other encounters with external reality, Lily often relies on scatological humor—so named for the Greek word for *dung* transliterated as *skat*—an ancient type of humor dating back at least as far as Aristophanes and the Greek comedy *The Frogs*.[31] Lily's favorite obscenity might be the word *shitbucket*, which she resorts to in the stressful time of springing Rosaleen from the hospital;[32]

or to simply pass judgment: "Eddie Hazelwurst. What a shitbuck-et."[33] She occasionally leaves off the "bucket" part: Lily is infuriat-ed when she and Zach stop near the Dixie Café, and she realizes how close the café is to the Tri-County Livestock Company. She wants to "scream out the window, 'Eat your damned breakfast grits somewhere else, why don't you? There's cow shit in the air! The way people lived their lives, settling for grits and cow shit, made me sick. My eyes stung all around the sockets."[34] That said, Lily's scatological references are not just about dung. When June frustrates her, Lily would like to feel superior. However, as she is urinating, she acknowledges, "There was no difference between my piss and June's. . . . Piss was piss."[35] Somewhat later, she ob-serves, "It's always a relief to empty your bladder. Better than sex, that's what Rosaleen said. As good as it felt, I sincerely hoped she was wrong."[36] When they discuss presidential candidates, Lily and Rosaleen share a joke at the expense of Barry Goldwater. Rosaleen was "not voting for Mr. Pisswater. . . . Goldwater, Pisswater, get it?"[37] Lily may be a daydreamer at times, but she never shirks re-ality and the grit and grime of life. To a large extent, just calling things what they are, even if just to herself, requires the courage she displays in her humor.

Bryant notes that scatological humor along with social satire have always constituted an intrinsic part of southern humor,[38] and in that sense Kidd does not disappoint, and neither does Lily, as she adopts the potty mouth of her authority figure, her father, revealing how her diversion from the sacred cow of soft-spoken, submissive, and polite femininity is something she has come by honestly. She has managed to voice her resentment, scorn, and even vulgarity that flies in the face of social expectation but cannot be discounted, as this is her own first person narrative. Having inherited her scat-ological language from a brutal parent, she escapes with only em-pathy for her child-self, and the result is both funny and poignant.

Kidd sets the novel during the turbulent 1960s civil rights era, and Lily often has a humorously perceptive take on segregation and race relations in the South. Tiburon townsfolk hear that Hollywood actor Jack Palance is coming to town to visit his sister and "bringing a colored woman with him."[39] The Boatwright family hears this rumor while they are enjoying a meal of pork chops and fried okra. August suddenly decides to send the overly empathetic May to the garden to pick tomatoes. Lily observes, "I could tell she [August] was afraid Jack Palance trying to integrate the movie theater might ruin May's okra feast."[40] In the context of the Palance paranoia, Lily continues to critique her own South: "[T]here is no greater affliction for the southern mind than people up north coming down to fix our way of life."[41] Such ironic commentaries make clear how Kidd, like other southern writers, expresses, via the satirical voice of Lily's inner monologue, the reality of injustices ignored and even reinforced in the South as well as "the enduring strength of southern women—black as well as white—whereby they have withstood the indignities imposed upon them and quietly provided the cohesive force without which their male-dominated society must surely have collapsed."[42]

Moreover, the scatological humor in *The Secret Life of Bees* includes religious satire as well. Kidd joins contemporary women writers who Bryant says "reject the outdated moral codes that for decades have restrained them" with "open indulgence in scatology [derived] from that rejection, too, as does their unrestrained ridicule of the taboos and sacred cows of southern evangelical Protestantism."[43] Some of Lily's sharpest barbs fly when she tries to understand and assess religion, including its praxis and institutions. Her hometown of Sylvan has no Catholics, "only Baptists and Methodists—but we got instructions in case we met them in our travels. . . . The church gave us a plastic glove with each step [of the five-part plan of salvation] written on a different finger. . . . Some ladies carried their salvation gloves in their purse in case they ran into a Catholic unexpectedly."[44] After Lily converts to the Boatwrights' religion with its Black Madonna, Lily recalls, "We didn't really allow Mary at our church [in Sylvan except at Christmas]."[45]

As Lily struggles with the realities of race and religion, her insights are often satirical if not outright sacrilegious, but no less hilarious. She recalls: "Every time a rumor got going about a group of Negroes coming to worship with us on Sunday morning, the deacons stood locked-arms . . . to turn them away. We loved them in the Lord, Brother Gerald said, but they had their own places."[46] When Lily shows Rosaleen the picture of the black Virgin Mary, Lily speculates about Rosaleen's thoughts: "*If Jesus's mother is black, how come we only know about the white Mary?*"[47] Then, Lily extends the thought with her own jab: "This would be like women finding out Jesus had had a twin sister who'd gotten half God's genes but none of the glory."[48]

Lily grapples with biblical accounts of miracles: "Later my mind would remember the plagues God had been *fond of sending early in his career* [emphasis added], the ones designed to make the pharaoh change his mind and let Moses take the people out of Egypt."[49] Lily ponders "this fascinating question: if you could have one miracle from the Bible happen to you, what would it be? . . . I thought walking on water would be interesting, but what good was that? I mean, you walk on water, what's the point?"[50] These musings indicate a healthy skepticism on Lily's part, and its blunt and unapologetic delivery becomes humorous.

Lily copes with Lily. In the spirit of Oscar Wilde's insight that "people are never so trivial as when they take themselves too seriously,"[51] Lily confronts herself with characteristic self-mockery, but not self-loathing. At times she can be a stereotypical adolescent focused on her own physical appearance. "I needed all the help that fashion could give me, since no one, not a single person, had ever said, 'Lily, you are such a pretty child,' except for Miss Jennings at church, and she was legally blind."[52] Lily believes charm school could transform her, but since she has no mother or grandmother, the school bars her from entering, an action that upsets Lily to the point that she vomits into the sink. Rosaleen taunts, "'What about vomit in a sink? They teach a charming way to do that?' . . . Sometimes I purely hated her," Lily claims.[53] Lily continues to confess: "After we read Ralph Waldo Emerson in class, I wrote 'My Philosophy of Life,' which I intended for the start of a book but could get only three pages out of it. Mrs. Henry said I needed to live past fourteen years old before I would have a philosophy."[54] When Lily meets Zachary Lincoln Taylor, she learns that his outstanding athletic ability could win him a scholarship. She describes her own poorer prospects: "This [Zach's ability] struck me as better than I would manage, since I was probably headed for beauty school now."[55] Lily is not commenting on her own beauty.

Lily is a realist. Throughout the novel Lily proves herself an accomplished liar in the tradition of Huck Finn and Moll Flanders, using bits of convenient truth. For instance, she creates a grandmother named Rose, "reading it off the snuff can."[56] Though she is resourceful with the fabrication, Lily also mocks her own lying when she inadvertently blabs the truth: "Any other day of my life I could have won a fibbing contest hands down, and that, *that* is what I came up with: the pathetic truth."[57] Quickly recovering, Lily continues to lie with the explanation of Rosaleen's bruises, "Caught her foot in the rug at the top of the stairs, the one my mother hooked herself."[58] Lily then seems to congratulate herself: "The secret of a good lie is don't overly explain, and throw in one good detail."[59] Although Lily is an inveterate liar, she exhibits enough conscience at least to be uncomfortable in her lies, sometimes: "*Lord God somebody stop me.*"[60] The self-awareness displayed is key to her survival. Without it and the ability to see herself as laughable by acknowledging the truth of her lying, which ironically requires relinquishing any ego she might have mustered amid all the meanness, she would be at risk for living a lie, having no sense of authentic worth at all. Without it, it is arguable there would be no Lily at all, and she would be a shell of a person with no humanity and no voice, simply mimicking or mirroring the external culture and circumstance around her. Such humor is for Lily "a tactic of personal survival,"[61] a dynamic appearing particularly in female humor.

That said, after the overly empathetic May Boatwright commits suicide, Lily's ability to cope with her own internal reality meets a severe challenge. Lily sinks into depression, stating, "Sometimes I didn't even feel like getting out of bed. I took to wearing my days-of-the-week panties out of order. It could be Monday and I'd have on underwear saying Thursday. I just didn't care."[62] Certainly Lily is depressed, as is the entire extended Boatwright family. However, the ironic juxtaposition of depression and disorganized underwear again creates an effect that prevents readers from being depressed, as Lily is able to find the comedy in the tragedy, preserving herself also from sinking into despair.

In *Man's Search for Meaning,* Victor Frankl described a survival technique from Auschwitz and Dachau: "Humor was another of the soul's weapons in the fight for self-preservation."[63] Although Lily Owens is a fictional character and although her often painful life does not approach the horrors Frankl endured, she has discovered and developed a weapon for her soul's preservation. Whether in one-liners such as the shitbucket reference or in the more layered humor of the Jack Palance anecdote, Lily finds her balance in humor and keeps herself together. She seems to sum up her coping approach in her comment at May's wake, when June plays her sister's theme song, "Oh! Susanna": "There's nothing like a small joke at a vigil to help you relax."[64] In this sense this humorous comment about humor is serious business for this character and this writer. It is a "complicated sense of joy,"[65] not unlike other southern women novelists, Eudora Welty among them, that Kidd brings. This connection between humor and empathy, a tragic feeling expressed in laughter, which can release even unbearable pathos,[66] could describe Kidd as well. "An empathetic vision that combines the recognition of the tragic with apprehension of the comic, a vision which the novel suggests is crucial for her emotional survival"[67] places Kidd also as another noteworthy southern female writer, who focuses on how voicing the truth can preserve one's humanity.

NOTES

1. Jennifer Hughes, "The South, Humor and Race," *Southern Literary Journal* 47, no. 1 (Fall 2014): 120, *EBSCOhost*, doi:10.1353/slj.2014.0024.
2. J. A. Bryant, Jr., "Woman in the Postmodern South," *Sewanee Review* 108, no. 2 (Spring 2000): 2, *EBSCOhost*, search.ebscohost.com/login.aspx?direct=true&db=a9h&AN=3344434&site=eds-live.
3. Bryant, "Woman in the Postmodern South," 2.
4. Bryant, "Woman in the Postmodern South," 2.
5. Sue Monk Kidd, *The Secret Life of Bees* (New York: Penguin Books, 2002), 16.
6. Humor studies range from academic formality to Internet informality, as noted in the following: According to their website, www.humorstudies.org, The International Society for Humor Studies (ISHS) "is a scholarly and professional organization dedicated to the advancement of humor research." The Society publishes *Humor: The International Journal of Humor Research* under the at-large editorship of Salvatore Attardo. The journal was "established as an international interdisciplinary forum for the publication of high-quality research papers on humor as an important and universal human faculty" and "draws upon a wide range of academic disciplines including anthropology, biology, computer science, education, family science, film studies, history, linguistics, literature, mathematics, medicine, philosophy, physiology, psychology, and sociology." More informally, www.laughteronlineuniversity.com offers a course in Laughter Therapy.
7. Eileen Gillooly, "Women and Humor," *Feminist Studies* 17, no. 3 (Fall 1991): 3, *EBSCOhost*, doi:10.2307/3178286.
8. Kidd, *The Secret Life of Bees,* p. 3.
9. Gillooly, "Women and Humor," 3.
10. Gillooly, "Women and Humor," 8.
11. Gillooly, "Women and Humor," 13.
12. Gillooly, "Women and Humor," 3.
13. Kidd, *The Secret Life of Bees*, 3.
14. Kidd, *The Secret Life of Bees*, 3.
15. Gillooly, "Women and Humor," 7.
16. Gillooly, "Women and Humor," 7.
17. Kidd, *The Secret Life of Bees*, 27.
18. Gillooly, "Women and Humor," 4.
19. Kidd, *The Secret Life of Bees,* 160.
20. Kidd, *The Secret Life of Bees,* 159.

21. John Morreall, *Taking Laughter Seriously* (Albany: State University of New York Press, 1983) *eBook Collection (EBSCOhost)*, EBSCOhost, accessed March 12, 2018.
22. Bryant, "Woman in the Postmodern South," 2.
23. Bryant, "Woman in the Postmodern South," 2.
24. Bryant, "Woman in the Postmodern South," 3.
25. Kidd, *The Secret Life of Bees,* 290.
26. Kidd, *The Secret Life of Bees,* 290.
27. Kidd, *The Secret Life of Bees,* 292.
28. Kidd, *The Secret Life of Bees,* 2-3.
29. Adrienne V. Akins, "'We Weren't Laughing at Them. . . .We're Grieving with You': Empathy and Comic Vision in Welty's 'The Optimist's Daughter,'" *Southern Literary Journal* 43, no. 2 (Spring 2011): 87, *EBSCOhost*, doi:10.1353/slj.2011.0009.
30. Akins, "'We Weren't Laughing at Them. . . .We're Grieving with You,'" 88.
31. Gilbert Murray, *Aristophanes: A Study* (New York: Oxford, 1933, 1965), 118-134.
32. Kidd, *The Secret Life of Bees,* 48.
33. Kidd, *The Secret Life of Bees*, 209.
34. Kidd, *The Secret Life of Bees*, 128.
35. Kidd, *The Secret Life of Bees*, 88.
36. Kidd, *The Secret Life of Bees*, 163.
37. Kidd, *The Secret Life of Bees*, 283.
38. Bryant, "Woman in the Postmodern South," 3.
39. Kidd, *The Secret Life of Bees*, 154.
40. Kidd, *The Secret Life of Bees*, 154.
41. Kidd, *The Secret Life of Bees*, 155.
42. Bryant, "Woman in the Postmodern South," 3.
43. Bryant, "Woman in the Postmodern South," 3.
44. Kidd, *The Secret Life of Bees,* 58.
45. Kidd, *The Secret Life of Bees*, 220.
46. Kidd, *The Secret Life of Bees*, 30.
47. Kidd, *The Secret Life of Bees*, 52.
48. Kidd, *The Secret Life of Bees*, 52.
49. Kidd, *The Secret Life of Bees*, 151.
50. Kidd, *The Secret Life of Bees*, 271.
51. Hesketh Pearson, *Oscar Wilde: His Life and Wit* (London: Harper & Brothers, 1946), 110.
52. Kidd, *The Secret Life of Bees*, 8.
53. Kidd, *The Secret Life of Bees*, 10.

54. Kidd, *The Secret Life of Bees*, 16.
55. Kidd, *The Secret Life of Bees*, 117.
56. Kidd, *The Secret Life of Bees*, 63.
57. Kidd, *The Secret Life of Bees*, 72.
58. Kidd, *The Secret Life of Bees*, 76.
59. Kidd, *The Secret Life of Bees*, 76.
60. Kidd, *The Secret Life of Bees*, 197.
61. Gillooly, "Women and Humor," 8.
62. Kidd, *The Secret Life of Bees*, 215.
63. Victor Frankl, *Man's Search for Meaning* (New York: Simon and Schuster, 1984), 63.
64. Kidd, *The Secret Life of Bees*, 200.
65. Akins, "'We Weren't Laughing at Them. . . .We're Grieving with You,'" 87.
66. Akins, "'We Weren't Laughing at Them. . . .We're Grieving with You,'" 88.
67. Akins, "'We Weren't Laughing at Them. . . .We're Grieving with You,'" 90.

BIBLIOGRAPHY

Akins, Adrienne V. "'We Weren't Laughing at Them. . . . We're Grieving with You': Empathy and Comic Vision in Welty's 'The Optimist's Daughter.'" *Southern Literary Journal* 43, no. 2 (Spring 2011): 87–104. *EBSCOhost*, doi:10.1353/slj.2011.0009.

Bryant, Jr., J. A. "Woman in the Postmodern South." *Sewanee Review* 108, no. 2 (Spring 2000): Lv. *EBSCOhost*, search.ebscohost.com/login.aspx?direct=true&db=a9h&AN=3344434&site=eds-live.

Frankl, Victor. *Man's Search for Meaning*. New York: Simon and Schuster, 1984.

Gillooly, Eileen. "Women and Humor." *Feminist Studies* 17, no. 3 (Fall 1991): 473. *EBSCOhost*, doi:10.2307/3178286.

Hughes, Jennifer. "The South, Humor and Race." *Southern Literary Journal* 47, no. 1 (Fall 2014): 120–124. *EBSCOhost*, doi:10.1353/slj.2014.0024.

Humor: The International Journal of Humor Research. www.humorstudies.org.

Kidd, Sue Monk. *The Secret Life of Bees*. New York: Penguin Books, 2002.

Morreall, John. *Taking Laughter Seriously*. Albany: State University of New York Press, 1983. *eBook Collection (EBSCOhost)*, EBSCOhost (accessed March 12, 2018).

Murray, Gilbert. *Aristophanes: A Study*. New York: Oxford, 1933, 1965.

Pearson, Hesketh. *Oscar Wilde: His Life and Wit*. London: Harper & Brothers, 1946. www.laughteronlineuniversity.com.

SEVEN

A Thread of Her Own:
The Book of Longings

DEBORAH J. KUHLMANN

*T*he *Book of Longings* is arguably a culmination of Sue
Monk Kidd's writings and is itself about writing. In fact,
all the threads that run throughout her works are present
here, providing a rich allegorical tapestry about the weaving, if you
will, or process of writing itself. Longing to write is where it begins
in the heart of her protagonist Ana, and the novel in that sense is
somewhat self-reflective, writing about writing as the fulfillment of
the heart's desire. Writing is itself a longing that begins in the imagination of the writer. Throughout the novel writing, and really all
things in Kidd's worldview, are in process. The pages are filled with
the present progressive tense, evoking a perspective that sees life
always as a state of becoming, *being* in motion and vitality, which
both the character and the reader are asked to embrace.

When Ana first sees Jesus, she is taken by his state of being, and
so much so that when she notices the red thread that drops from
his garment, she immediately places it around her wrist, and there
it remains. It is a thread that runs throughout the novel, symboliz-
ing that love is at the heart of the story, perhaps even every story of
Kidd's. It is after all from the heart's longing that writing comes for

both Ana, the protagonist writer, and the novel writer Kidd herself. Perhaps it is even a suggestion that love is the source of all art, all craft, all writing. Simultaneously it is also suggestive of all of the "threads" that go into the writing process in general and also into Kidd's particular writing. In *The Book of Longings* the reader will find all of the threads, if you will, that are found in her previous works as well. But in this text this author brings the most audacious and expanded rendering of those threads to date.

Kidd has had other female protagonists who fell in love with men of faith, such as the monk in *The Mermaid Chair* or the devout Quaker Israel Morris in *The Invention of Wings*. But this time Kidd has her main character fall in love with Jesus himself. If there have been spiritual threads in all of her earlier novels and specifically ones that lean on contemplative Christianity, this time this writer takes on the most provocative stand possible to face Christian tradition with what could easily be termed feminist theology. The novel is grounded in Christology, even celebrating the life of Jesus and his teachings, but it is his wife Ana, herself an imaginary possibility that could be seen as downright blasphemous by some, who is the voice that could subvert the patriarchal version of Christianity, even if just to suggest there could be another "version" than the one in the biblical canon. At the end of the novel Kidd devotes several pages to what could be termed a disclaimer, giving an explanation of the origins of her imaginary character with all due respect for Christianity but owning her reasons—should I say birthright—to such creativity. On the one hand, it confronts the purity of Jesus, if you will, in the sense that this woman is a physical lover of Jesus, but on the other, it is hard to argue with the fact that she loves Jesus emotionally and spiritually. Love is again at the heart of it all, and that is the thread, the red thread that runs throughout this work.

That said, while Kidd does not abandon the Christian theology in which so much of her work is rooted, she does assert a feminist Christian theology, as she gives Ana what Joy Ann McDougall in "Rising with Mary: Re-visioning a Feminist Theology of the Cross and Resurrection" calls "the power to speak": to speak a Word on behalf of life, a word of protest against the squandering of women's gifts, a word of affirmation for challenges met, and a word of visionary hope that counters the familiar faces of gender oppression."[1] Kidd herself says of the day Ana appeared in her imagination that she knew "one thing about her besides her name. I knew what she wanted most was a voice."[2] As in other Kidd novels, this is yet another journey of the protagonist coming to herself and finding her voice, and it is a spiritual experience that is rooted in being, by being both with herself and with her beloved Jesus. In this way Kidd's character resonates with McDougall's point, that

> first, there is the basic insight that coming to one's self occurs in the presence of God and as a gift of God, in which we see ourselves held fast as the precious children of God, as recipients of an inexhaustible and faithful love in the midst of the deepest deceptions and disappointments of human life. This is a deeply edifying truth because it grants to women a clear vision of one's goodness and inviolable worth in the midst of a myriad of gender distortions and destructive forces.[3]

The female voice is pivotal and central in all of Kidd's works, but what has to precede writing or speaking is always a way of knowing, and so epistemology is another important thread in her novels. Again, all things in Kidd's created worlds are a process, and expressed in a progressive tense is knowing and all of its counterparts, such as questioning, seeing, intuiting, empathizing, choosing, freeing, writing, and healing. "Could we know the ways of God or not?"[4] "Why would God send . . . a vision if it has no meaning other than what I give to it?"[5] "Did he possess an intention for us, his people, as religion believed, or was it up to us to invent meaning for ourselves?"[6] What are the ways of God to woman? What is the difference between choosing God and the "largeness"[7] that is the longing found within the self? Can a person's intuition be the vehicle to knowing, as it is for Ana and as it has been for previous protagonists of Kidd's, such as Lily in *The Secret Life of Bees* and Sarah in *The Invention of Wings*? Visions and dreams, seeing on a deeper level than the physical appearance of creation, and knowing then what to choose, all inform the intuition that is in a Kidd world the highest form of intelligence, surpassing logic and reason as ways of understanding. This is what informs the authentic voice of Ana from this writer.

Writing, too, is a way to understanding, as it uncovers or discovers what is possible, which is always informed by an empathetic imagination for Kidd. In "The Inscribed Heart: A Spirituality of Intellectual Work: Writing as a Spiritual Practice," Stephanie Paulsell makes a relevant note when she says that "practicing writing as a spiritual discipline requires acts of faith and imagination: we must care about our readers, no matter how anonymous they are."[8] She even cites Virginia Woolf when she says that

> we must, like Woolf, discover in our writing how to reunite
> what has been severed, to connect what seems disparate, to
> create out of a diversity of material and perspective some new
> thing. Writers are lovers, Woolf suggests in *To the Lighthouse*.
> "There might be lovers whose gift it was to choose out the
> elements of things and place them together and so, giving them
> a wholeness not theirs in life, make of some scene, or meeting
> of people (all now gone and separate), one of those globed
> compacted things over which thought lingers and love plays."[9]

It is interesting that when she wrote *The Book of Longings*, Kidd took inspiration from Virginia Woolf, who said "Everything is the proper stuff of fiction."[10] Ana, her character, dares to write about everything, and particularly about those people and things that have been left unsaid and unseen, in order to better understand. She is a lover.

Yaltha, Ana's aunt, who serves as the wise woman, mentor, even priestess figure, tells her to "write what's inside here, inside your holy of holies," tapping her heart.[11] Perhaps what could be a frame for the entire book, Yaltha also tells Ana that "a man's holy of holies contains God's laws, but inside a woman there are only longings."[12] But such longings are not appetites. They are gifts from God. It is what Ana calls the largeness in her. It is the light in her that she believes can shine.[13] Ana writes her prayer "Lord our God, hear my prayer, the prayer of my heart. Bless the largeness inside me, no matter how I fear it. Bless my reed pens and my inks. Bless the words I write. May they be beautiful in your sight. May they be visible to eyes not yet born."[14] Yaltha again has told Ana that "when the longing of one's heart is inked into words and offered as a prayer, that's when it springs to life in God's mind."[15] She continues to counsel Ana, "Return to your longing. It will teach you everything."[16] Clearly, this longing is an intelligence that is a teacher and guide for one's life, not mere gratification.

When Ana faces the prospects of losing her scrolls, vials of ink, reed pens, sheets of papyrus, and her incantation bowl, she acknowledges how "they also held the full weight of my craving to express myself, to lift out of my small self, out of the enclosure of my life, and find what lay beyond. I wanted for so much."[17] Ana is longing for her full humanity and to be herself in a world that could deny her that. But she is at the same time longing for that which is greater than self. She longs to write the unwritten stories of women. She longs to be the voice that she is not just for her own sake, but to be the voice of those who have been voiceless and invisible. Her being as a writer, this way of being in her, is born of love. Again, Paulsell in her article on writing as a spiritual practice itself declares that there exists

> an irreplaceable chance for us to grow intimate with language, to find a voice that's true, to write in a way that betrays our love. If we embrace writing as a spiritual practice, it will bear fruit in every form of our ministries: in our scholarship, in our sermons, in our liturgies and prayers. If we write from any other motive than to find out what belongs to what, or to heal and reunite, or to reach across boundaries, or to seek communion with others, or to respond to what is written on our hearts, or to peel back the cotton wool of nonbeing, or to seek the real behind appearances, or to illuminate invisible connections, or

to open a path between solitude and community, or to find God, then writing will not change us. Nor will be known the rapture Virginia Woolf speaks of, or the deep understanding Marguerite d'Oingt describes. The very best writing emerges from generosity, the desire to meet and nourish another. No matter how inadequate our words may seem to us, in our struggle to find the right ones, we make room for others to find words of their own.[18]

She could be speaking of Sue Monk Kidd, the author, or her character Ana, and certainly the way that Kidd depicts the process of writing here in *The Book of Longings*.

More threads in Kidd's novel definitely intertwine and the same weaving of them, if you will, has appeared in earlier writings as well. Two that are prominent are identity and being, but in *The Book of Longings* identity is actually expressed **in being**, more specifically alluding to the biblical scripture in Exodus 3:14, when God declares in a holy moment with Moses saying "I AM THAT I AM," i. e. pure being, strewn throughout the text as Ana herself declares who she is in numerous "I am" statements. Moreover, not only identity but the greatest love itself is mirrored in those moments when Jesus or Ana or Tabitha or Yaltha declare to one another "I am with you," i.e., I am "being with" you. The opening statement begins the thread of "I ams," when the protagonist begins "I am Ana."[19] It is "in this being together" with Jesus where Ana finds rapture.[20] And as they break bread together she finds "the first tiny sprout of . . . belonging."[21] It is arguable that for all of the times Yaltha counsels Ana with her worldly guidance that she must make her own freedom, and similarly her vision "will mean what [she] makes it to mean,"[22] most nourishing of all is when Yaltha says to Ana simply "I'm here."[23] For Kidd it is in being where love and power and truth reside.

Perhaps most revealing of all is when Ana voices her own beliefs that "God could be love, as Jesus believed. . . . [but] For me, he would be I Am Who I Am, the beingness in our midst."[24] Kidd does not oversimplify this "theology of beingness," as through Ana she leans on, is informed by, and validates Christianity's premise that God is Love. Just as she does recognize the struggle or conflict to choose the largeness of self or to choose God over and above the small self, for Kidd they are ultimately not separate but are part of the same being. So when Yaltha reminds her to make her own meaning, Ana hears the ring of truth in that, as making meaning in writing is her craft for which she longs, but she also believes such a seed was planted in her by her Creator. In Ana's conversation with Jesus she declares to him that God's kingdom is "a place inside us."[25] And this Jesus responds with "So I believe."[26] Ana follows, "Then does God live in the Temple in Jerusalem or in this king- dom inside us?" "Can he not live in both?" he asks. She responds, "Can he not live everywhere?"[27] Ana finds reassurance in this to think of God "as an essence that lived everywhere."[28] And together they agree that "God cannot be contained," that they can "set him free"[29] to **Be** God.

When Ana finds Tabitha again after her tongue has been muti- lated, the first thing she says to her is simply "I'm here."[30] When Ana loses her child Susanna, she imagines what she will say to Jesus, that she "loved her the way you love God, with all my heart and soul and might";[31] she loved her with her whole being. And when Jesus does return to learn of the child's death, he says to Ana, "I should've been with you."[32] For Kidd "being with" another is perhaps the highest form of being, for this is love. Being is where God resides. So, when we be ourselves, it is good, and when we be with another in their suffering and their joy, it is even better. Such is the theology of being from Sue Monk Kidd in her *Book of Longings*.

Another thread existing throughout the book are the writ- ings within the writing, such as the poem "The Thunder: Perfect Mind," which expresses the paradoxical I AMs and thus begins the tribute to being whole at the beginning of this novel. We later learn Kidd has taken poetic license to attribute the authorship, which is unknown, to Ana. "I am the first and the last" is her opening declaration that she is the incorporation or embodiment of all. Not unlike Walt Whitman's "Song of Myself," in saying who she is, she refutes being one thing or another and thereby will not be identified by a mere label nor will she have her humanity reduced. "I am she who is honored and she who is mocked." She is both. She establishes a prism of paradox as the lens through which she should be seen, asserting her visibility over the invisibility that too often haunts the story told about herself and other women. "I am the whore and the holy woman. I am the wife and the virgin. I am the mother and the daughter. I am she . . . " Ana's prayer as well alludes to this degree of wholeness and irreducibility in her: "Lord, our God, hear my prayer, the prayer of my heart. Bless the largeness inside me, no matter how I fear it."[33] And again, much later in her prayer to Sophia, Breath of God, she prays for deliverance "To the place I will be born,"[34] expressing her longing for the self's fulfillment, life, and wholeness. It is herself that is drawn to Jesus, so the seeming opposing longings within her to follow Jesus and to follow the longing of her self's highest calling would be in conflict, but they are not. They are one. They are both present in her being who she is. Even Jesus blesses that "largeness" within her,[35] as he knows he, too, will follow the largeness that God has bestowed on himself as well.

Could these be necessary paradoxes? In "Redressing the Past, Doing Justice in the Present: Necessary Paradoxes" Tanya van Wyk identifies paradox as a response to the postcolonial dilemma of binary thinking, saying "Paradoxes do not make sense and we would want to 'settle' them. Embracing their tension, however, might just help us to live, creatively, collectively, and help us to nourish in the midst of our *broken whole*—our beautiful mosaic."[36] Likewise, Kidd's vision of truth born of paradoxical unity reveals the simultaneous longing for loving self and to love the other, even that which is greater than self. Moreover, such a dilemma is not divorced from the postcolonial longing for individual identity and for collective unity. Theologian Tanya van Wyk mirrors in this sense Kidd's invitation to willingly embrace both difference and sameness in creative tension, rather than remaining stuck in polarization and binary categories that restrict making space for possibility, authenticity, and even humanity. She cites Denise Ackermann's *Surprised by the Man on the Borrowed Donkey* to describe

> a paradox as a statement that seems self-contradictory or absurd, but in reality it expresses a possible truth. For her, a paradox promises that apparent opposites can come together in our lives and that *either/or* thinking can be replaced with something that is closer to *both/and* (Ackermann 2014:55). . . . Ackermann's notion of paradox as a departure point [reflects] what I think are necessary conditions for collective living and reconciling diversity—authentic transformation—in an era that demands it, longs for it and needs it. I do this in an attempt to move further away from division and polarisation and closer to the promise of the restoration in the form of *both/and* . . . [a] theology (and spirituality) [that] has a certain *spaciousness* for *holding* the *tension* of opposites to flourish amidst the human condition.[37]

It would be easy to place Kidd's theology, if you will, or way of being as seen through the lens of paradoxes in postcolonial concert with both van Wyk and Ackermann.

Ultimately, though, it is a healing and a homecoming to both self and the divine, interwoven threads in Kidd's perspective, where Ana finds her belonging at last. Ana says she "longed not only for him, but for myself."[38] When her fear of what will happen to Jesus overcomes her, Yaltha comforts her, "When I tell you all shall be well, I don't mean life won't bring you tragedy. Life will be life. I only mean you will be well in spite of it. All shall be well, **no matter what.**"[39] Again, the paradox and making space for both what is broken and what cannot be broken emerges. "There's a place in you that is inviolate—it's the surest part of you, a piece of Sophia herself," Yaltha, the wise woman, asserts.[40] Ana is on the road to being at home both with herself and that which is larger than herself, and it is divine. It is healing. She and her aunt even find sanctuary with the Therapeutae, an early Christian monastery, whose monks held to the notion that worship was restorative, even a cure. There Ana can pursue what is seen as spiritual work, her longing for "study, reading, writing, composing songs, prayer," and so on, among those who dwell there "out of love for a quiet, contemplative life. They come to study and to keep the memory of God alive."[41] One epiphany that comes to her while she is there is that all things may be holy, that all is sacred.[42] Here she makes her book. Here she comes to "no longer [believe] in the God of rescue, only the God of presence,"[43] again a theology of being for Kidd. And here emerges the last stage of her writing process, and that is her longing to be read.

Ana declares after the death of Jesus that he "had been my home."[44] This author in no way dismisses and in fact affirms the power of the Christ in this way. But with him gone, Ana recognizes that her "home was on a hillside in Egypt" with the Therapeutae.[45] She even says it felt like a "homecoming."[46] When she tries to tell the women about this community, she admits how she "felt the longing in me for home" rising up in her. And again, as she sets out on her journey there, she paradoxically felt "the happiness of home-going" that "was lodged beside [her] sorrow."[47] Once back with the Therapeutae with Yaltha and Tabitha, she discovers how they had somehow even shaped themselves into "a family."[48] Moreover, Jesus appears to her there, saying "I never left"[49] and "I will always be with you."[50] I will always **BE** with you, and then Ana knows Jesus is with her, is in her, and so the task before her becomes finding a way to preserve her writings. At Yaltha's advice, in a rich irony, she buries them in the hillside, so they can one day be found again:

> Stories of matriarchs; the rape and maiming of Tabitha; the
> terrors men inflicted on women; the cruelties of Antipas;
> the braveries of Phasaelis; my marriage to Jesus; the death of
> Susanna; the exile of Yaltha; the enslavement of Diodora; the
> power of Sophia; the story of Isis; **Thunder: Perfect Mind**; and
> a plethora of other ideas about women that turned traditionally
> held beliefs upside down.[52]

To write these writings has been her own way home as much as they are meant as a way to give other women a visibility and a voice, a home, too. Longing for the love of herself and her neighbor, longing for the love of Jesus and herself, longing to express what is in her, longing for love of this life and all that is sacred comprise all the threads of writing that inhabit this *Book of Longings*. Following the "largeness" that is within her, that is, to be who she is, brings her home internally and spiritually. For Kidd to do that is not selfish or profane. It is the road to fulfillment and purpose, and it is a spiritual journey. Life is that. Being is that. And that is reiterated externally, when Ana declares her own reality at the end, "I am a voice."[52] She is at that moment every woman. She is the character and the author, the first and the last, the wife and the virgin, the mother and the daughter, the whore and the holy woman. She is whole. She has made "her own quest—that of following her longings in pursuit of the largeness inside herself."[53] And it is more than enough. As Kidd herself said, what she knew of Ana was that "what she wanted most was a voice."[54] She is longing to be that. She can now declare she is that. And when spoken, it is no less than healing, a coming home to self, a message then from Kidd's own voice to her readers. The self's being is sacred and interconnected to its Creator, a thread of her own, found at the heart of *The Book of Longings,* a tapestry of beauty and truth about being. Whether southern, American, postcolonial, gender-bending, or global, Kidd's work stands as a timeless read for all, this narrative about the process of becoming a fully human being.

NOTES

1. Joy Ann McDougall, "Rising with Mary: Re-Visioning a Feminist Theology of the Cross and Resurrection," *Theology Today* 69, no. 2 (2012): 75, doi:10.1177/0040573612446857.
2. Sue Monk Kidd, *The Book of Longings* (New York: Random House, 2020), 562.

3. McDougall, "Rising with Mary," 175.

4. McDougall, "Rising with Mary," 113.

5. McDougall, "Rising with Mary," 113.

6. McDougall, "Rising with Mary," 113.

7. Kidd, *The Book of Longings*, 17.

8. Stephanie Paulsell, "'The Inscribed Heart: A Spirituality of Intellectual Work': Writing as a Spiritual Practice," *Lexington Theological Quarterly* 36.3 (2001): 166, http://search.ebscohost.com.waylandbu.idm.oclc.org/login.aspx?direct=true&db=rfh&AN=ATLA0001343774&site=eds-live.

9. Paulsell, "'The Inscribed Heart: A Spirituality of Intellectual Work,'" 166-167.

10. Kidd, *The Book of Longings*, 553.

11. Kidd, *The Book of Longings*, 10.

12. Kidd, *The Book of Longings*, 10.

13. Kidd, *The Book of Longings*, 51.

14. Kidd, *The Book of Longings*, 17.

15. Kidd, *The Book of Longings*, 55.

16. Kidd, *The Book of Longings*, 55.

17. Kidd, *The Book of Longings*, 74.

18. Paulsell, "'The Inscribed Heart: A Spirituality of Intellectual Work,'" 168.

19. Kidd, *The Book of Longings*, 3.

20. Kidd, *The Book of Longings*, 118.

21. Kidd, *The Book of Longings*, 120.

22. Kidd, *The Book of Longings*, 112.

23. Kidd, *The Book of Longings*, 25.

24. Kidd, *The Book of Longings*, 166.

25. Kidd, *The Book of Longings*, 165.

26. Kidd, *The Book of Longings*, 166.

27. Kidd, *The Book of Longings*, 166.

28. Kidd, *The Book of Longings*, 166.

29. Kidd, *The Book of Longings*, 166.

30. Kidd, *The Book of Longings*, 224.

31. Kidd, *The Book of Longings*, 245.

32. Kidd, *The Book of Longings*, 254.

33. Kidd, *The Book of Longings*, 17.

34. Kidd, *The Book of Longings*, 339.

35. Kidd, *The Book of Longings*, 340.

36. Tanya van Wyk, "Redressing the Past, Doing Justice in the Present: Necessary Paradoxes," *Hervormde Teologiese Studies* 75.4 (2019): 8, doi:10.4102/hts.v75i4.5625.

37. van Wyk, "Redressing the Past, Doing Justice in the Present," 2.
38. Kidd, *The Book of Longings*, 360.
39. Kidd, *The Book of Longings*, 374.
40. Kidd, *The Book of Longings*, 374.
41. Kidd, *The Book of Longings*, 437.
42. Kidd, *The Book of Longings*, 349.
43. Kidd, *The Book of Longings*, 470.
44. Kidd, *The Book of Longings*, 529.
45. Kidd, *The Book of Longings*, 529.
46. Kidd, *The Book of Longings*, 529.
47. Kidd, *The Book of Longings*, 532.
48. Kidd, *The Book of Longings*, 541.
49. Kidd, *The Book of Longings*, 543.
50. Kidd, *The Book of Longings*, 544.
51. Kidd, *The Book of Longings*, 548-549.
52. Kidd, *The Book of Longings*, 551.
53. Kidd, *The Book of Longings*, 562.
54. Kidd, *The Book of Longings*, 562.

BIBLIOGRAPHY

Kidd, Sue Monk. *The Book of Longings*. New York: Random House, 2020.
McDougall, Joy Ann. "Rising with Mary: Re-Visioning a Feminist Theology of the Cross and Resurrection." *Theology Today* 69, no. 2 (2012): 166–76. doi:10.1177/0040573612446857.
Paulsell, Stephanie. "'The Inscribed Heart: A Spirituality of Intellectual Work': Writing as a Spiritual Practice." *Lexington Theological Quarterly* 36, no. 3 (2001): 155–69. http://search.ebscohost.com.waylandbu.idm.oclc.org/login.aspx?direct=true&db=rfh&AN=ATLA0001343774&site=eds-live.
The Holy Bible: King James Version. Peabody, MA: Hendrickson Publishers, 2003.
Van Wyk, Tanya. "Redressing the Past, Doing Justice in the Present: Necessary Paradoxes." *Hervormde Teologiese Studies* 75, no. 4 (2019): 1–9. doi:10.4102/hts.v75i4.5625.

ACKNOWLEDGMENTS

I mmense gratitude goes to my colleagues and fellow contributors, who first said yes to this collection and have continued to stay the course to its completion. I am tremendously thankful to Drs. Cindy McClenagan, Erin Heath, and Arch Mayfield for their insights and scholarship. As well, for Dr. Dan Williams, director of TCU Press, I am exceedingly grateful. His professionalism, direction, and support throughout the process to acceptance has been exceptional, as has been that of Molly Spain, assistant editor at TCU Press, who took up the task once publication was a certainty. The encouragement and kindness of Dr. Brent Lynn, director of WBU Writing Center at Wayland Baptist University, cannot go unmentioned. And most of all, my husband, Robert L. Johnson, has been my anchor in the inevitable waves of the process in ways too numerous to name.

CONTRIBUTORS

ERIN HEATH, PhD, is professor of English in the School of Languages and Literature at Wayland Baptist University in Plainview, Texas. She teaches courses in writing, literature, and film. Dr. Heath earned her PhD at University of Illinois in Urbana-Champaign. She holds both a master's and bachelor's degree in English from Texas Tech University. Her research interests are primarily in film and American literature.

DEBORAH J. KUHLMANN, PhD, joined Wayland Baptist University in 2009 and continues to be professor of English in the School of Languages and Literature, where she has taught undergraduate and graduate courses in writing and literature online. She holds a bachelor's degree from Texas Christian University and a master's degree from the University of Arkansas, and she completed her PhD in English at Texas Christian University in 1985. Dr. Kuhlmann's research interests gravitate toward epiphanies and epistemological themes in fiction as well as poetry.

CINDY M. McCLENAGAN, PhD, serves as vice president of Academic Affairs at Wayland Baptist University in Plainview, Texas, where she oversees all graduate and undergraduate academic programs to ensure quality and relevance. Dr. McClenagan holds a PhD in English from Texas Tech University, as well as a master's degree from the University of Iowa and a bachelor's degree from Luther College. A professor of English, her research presentations and publications include the fields of African American literature, violent women in American literature, young adult literature, and dystopian literature.

ARCH MAYFIELD, PhD, taught at Wayland Baptist University for many years. He earned a bachelor's degree in political science and a master's degree in English from Hardin-Simmons University. Dr. Mayfield's PhD in English is from Texas Tech University. He served as president of the Conference of College Teachers of English for 2012-2013. Dr. Mayfield now serves at Texas Christian University as a part-time professional writing consultant at the Center for Writing and teaches as adjunct faculty for the English Department.

CPSIA information can be obtained
at www.ICGtesting.com
Printed in the USA
JSHW020328030423
39758JS00001B/1

9 780875 658155